DISCERNMENT:
Seeking God
In Every Situation

Rev. Chris Aridas

LIVING FLAME PRESS
Locust Valley, N. Y. 11560

Cover Design: Robert Manning

Readings from the Jerusalem Bible, Copyright © 1966 by
Darton, Longman, & Todd, Ltd. and Doubleday & Company,
Inc. Used by permission of the publishers.

Nihil Obstat: Reverend John C. Meszaros, J.C.D.
Censor Librorum
June 26th, 1981

Imprimatur: Most Reverend John R. McGann, D.D.
Bishop of Rockville Centre
June 29th, 1981

Published by: Living Flame Press/Locust Valley/New York
11560

ISBN: 0-914544-37-3

Copyright: 1981 by Chris Aridas

Printed in the United States of America

Dedication

I dedicate this book to Mrs. Dot Horstman, Sister Mary Sullivan, r.c., Sister Agnes Forman, r.c., and the Cenacle Sisters in Lantana, Florida. Their prayers and encouragement provided me with the incentive to move beyond my own limitations. To them, a special ''Thank You'' is offered.

Acknowledgments

My sincerest thanks to the sisters and priests who reviewed the manuscript, corrected my faulty grammar, and clarified my obtuse prose: Sister Thelma Hall, r.c., Sister Patricia Horan, O.P., Sister Regina McAuley, S.J., Sister M. Brendan, RSHM, Mr. Douglas Michaud, Father Steve Peterson, and Father Joe Towle.

In addition, I am deeply grateful to my "brothers" William Boecker and Joseph Juhasz for the support and encouragement they offered while I struggled through the Discernment Workshop in Florida. Their contribution during that retreat gave me the confidence and inspiration to continue.

For their indispensable help, on the most practical of levels, I shall never cease to appreciate Mrs. Agnes Schomber's dedication and professionalism in typing the manuscript under a great deal of pressure, and Mr. Peter Reilly's efforts in preparing the final copies.

Table of Contents

Introduction

Blessed be the God and Father of our Lord Jesus Christ, who has blessed us with all the spiritual blessings of heaven in Christ. Before the world was made, he chose us, chose us in Christ, to be holy and spotless, and to live through love in his presence, determining that we should become his adopted sons, through Jesus Christ for his own kind purposes, to make us praise the glory of his grace, his free gift to us in the Beloved, in whom, through his blood, we gain our freedom, the forgiveness of our sins.

Such is the richness of the grace which he has showered on us in all wisdom and insight. He has let us know the mystery of his purpose, the hidden plan he so kindly made in Christ from the beginning to act upon when the times had run their course to the end: that he would bring everything together under Christ, as head, everything in the heavens and everything on earth. And it is in him that we were claimed as God's own, chosen from the beginning, under the predetermined plan of the one who guides all things as he decides by his own will; chosen to be, for his greater glory, the people who would put their hopes in Christ before he came. Now you too, in him, have heard the message of the truth and the good news of your salvation, and have believed it; and you too have been stamped with the seal of the Holy Spirit of the Promise, the pledge of our inheritance which brings freedom for those whom God has taken for his own, to make his glory praised.

(Ephesians 1:3-14)

Discernment is a fascinating subject. It broadens our horizon, challenges our faith, raises our hopes, seeks to allay our fears. We all want to know "how to discern," how to know God's will. Undoubtedly, you are hoping that this book might give you the answer — or at least provide a reasonable outline: which prayer to say, when to say it, and how to understand the answer.

Such a hope, however, will lead to disappointment, for that is not where DISCERNMENT: SEEKING GOD IN OUR EVERYDAY LIFE is going to take you. In reality, there is no magic prayer, no special time, no favored sign or gesture that reveals God's will for us — except Jesus. Jesus *is* the Father's will for us. Jesus, the Word of the Father spoken in time through the sign of a Virgin. He is the Father's will for us in every situation. Should you decide to continue, knowing that this will be the direction taken, begin by relaxing. Sit back; hum a hymn; quietly praise and thank the Father for making it as simple as a Word. Say the Word, "Jesus." Remember: it is through him that we are held in the arms of a loving Father, a Father who cares for us, loves us, and forgives us.

Perhaps you might want to pray a relaxing psalm. Two short ones are printed below. Pray one or the other, slowly, peacefully. Savor the words, the promises given, the hopes instilled.

> I wait for Yahweh, my soul waits for
>   him,
> I rely on his promise,
> my soul relies on the Lord
> more than a watchman on the coming
>   of dawn.
> Let Israel rely on Yahweh
> as much as the watchman on the dawn!
> For it is with Yahweh that mercy is to
>   be found,
> and a generous redemption;
> it is he who redeems Israel
> from all their sins. (Psalm 130:5-8)

> Yahweh, my heart has no lofty ambitions,
> my eyes do not look too high.
> I am not concerned with great affairs
> or marvels beyond my scope.
> Enough for me to keep my soul tranquil
>   and quiet
> like a child that has been weaned.

> Israel, rely on Yahweh,
> now and for always!

(Psalm 131)

We want to know about discernment, and the Lord wants to teach us. And so, continue to relax in prayer. Don't worry about what He might say or do. After all, we've been chosen and called His very own, so that the work *He* has begun in us can be brought to completion. We want to learn about discernment, so let's expect that He will teach us.

As we seek the Father's will, therefore, allow the Spirit to emerge from within. His power is there — the power of Jesus, the power of the Father's love — so expect to see it, and know it. He desires to surprise us with the Love that is within, so pray to be ready for the unexpected. Just as we need to be ready for the unexpected, just as we need to be ready to respond to a variety of gestures from our loved ones, so we need to be open to a variety of gestures from the Father. If the men on the road to Emmaus had been ready for the unexpected, they would have known the Father's will. They were not ready; they were bound to the routine. Jesus, however, desired to appear in an unexpected, yet ordinary way — through a simple conversation, and the sharing of bread. They did not learn the Father's will because they did not recognize His will, present to them in Jesus.

Finally, as we relax, and as we expect the surprise of the Father's love, we will learn his ways. Just as a child relaxes in his/her father's arms and expects to float, so too, can we learn how to swim in His Love by following the child's example, viz. trusting and relaxing. The Lord wants to teach us His will. Of this, be certain.

This text, however, can only point the way. It is the Father who must teach us; it is the Father, in Jesus, Who must take us; it is the Father, through the Spirit, Who must be our guide. And this He will do, as promised. He will meet us in His Son, Jesus (His will for us) and take us beyond to the Kingdom. For this reason the Word became flesh, so that the Father's will — Jesus, the Word of Love spoken from the Father's heart — could be made known. (cf. 1 John 1:1-4)

HOW TO READ THIS BOOK

The key to discernment is silence. To relax in the Father and to know His will, requires silence. What is said to you in this book is not important; what God gives you in silence, however, is important. It is in the stillness, the quiet voice, the whispers that we sense God's tuggings, pullings, and leadings. While reading this book, therefore, choose silence, for just as the Eternal Word emerged from the silence of Mary's womb, so will He emerge again in the silence of our hearts.

Be as generous with prayer as with silence. Suggested prayer exercises will be given after several chapters. Try to use the points given for meditation.

Finally, may I suggest that you begin your search for the Father's will by praying this prayer, or one similar in tone and theme:

> *Father, I have decided to follow your Son;*
> *I have decided to put aside everything, and*
>   *everyone*
> *so that I might know the consuming Love*
> *you desire to give me.*
> *Father, I have decided to choose your Son*
> *in every situation as best as I am able.*
> *I only ask that you grant me*
> *the grace and strength needed to make that*
>   *choice a reality.*
> *Let no barrier stand in my way;*
> *let no one and no thing come between us.*
> *Help me to keep my eyes, my heart, my*
>   *very being centered on you*
> *so I might enter into your life —*
> *a life shared with me in Jesus your Son.*
> *Father, grant me this grace*
> *so I may abide in your heart forever.*

THE GOAL

The goal of discernment is to find God, and in finding Him, to know His will. Note the sequence: we first seek Him, *then* His will. For many, this sequence is reversed. Time and energy are spent seeking to know what He wants us to do, rather than seeking Him alone. We do not have to accomplish something for Him to reveal His will to us; all we need do is seek Him to find His will.

The enterprise before us, therefore, has little to

14

do with accomplishments, and everything to do with discovery. For in discernment, we are meant to discover, uncover the wholeness and the holiness of God; to grasp the very essence of the Father as revealed to us in Jesus, His Word. Such a "discovery" eventually uncovers God's will for us because in grasping Him, we are grasped by Him. Just as a child leaps into a father's arms, and clings to the father who grasps him/her tightly, so we are called to leap towards our Heavenly Father so He might grasp us tightly.

Knowing the unknowable, or the hidden answer, therefore, has little to do with discernment. Rather than being a magic system which unveils God's plan, it is the concrete process of entering the Father's life by living the life of the Risen Lord. More than asking God to enter us, we — through a life of discernment — enter his life through Jesus, the One who is truly and totally alive in the Father.

Our entrance into Jesus' life takes place on a daily basis as we learn to recognize and identify our personal, spiritual movements: those inner promptings, attractions, etc. — often called emotions or affections — which are part of our ordinary, human experience. Unfortunately, we often seek the bolt of lightning, the mystical high, the pounding of the heart when trying to recognize the Father's will. True discernment, however, does not wait for the extraordinary, but roots itself in our ordinary, human experience. We can make this assumption because the extraordinary, i.e. Jesus, in taking on our flesh, *has become ordinary* (human).

Discernment, therefore, is surprisingly practical. It is the recognition of God's voice and call spoken here and now in the ordinary, everyday experience of our humanity, rather than in the esoteric, god-talk whispered in our ear during some transcendental moment.

This "human" approach to discernment should not surprise us. After all, we were made to converse with the Father who speaks His complete Word to us in the Incarnate Lord. God's language, therefore, His method of dialogue, will not be in some indecipherable code which few can comprehend. In fact, He has already chosen His language by speaking to us in the one, common denominator of our humanity — as it is lived by Christ.

In our humanity, therefore, God's will can be found, because Jesus, His will for us, has entered into that humanity. This reality is meant to free us. Now, we can look within and find God whose Word dwells in our human-ness.

Yet, God's Word does not dwell in a vacuum. Mingled with the Word, are those words and phrases which do not find their base in the Father. True discernment, therefore, should teach us to inspect our inner words against the proper goal of our life, namely, choosing the Father through Jesus. More than asking whether God is leading us through our affections and inner feelings, we can now ask whether these inner feelings and emotions are leading us to God!

Discernment, then, is that ongoing process of conversion and transformation which separates the Eternal Word within, from the emotions and affections which prevent that Word from being heard. This process, nurtured by faith, helps us to live in the Kingdom by choosing Jesus.

By learning to live a life of discernment, we will find our human experiences pregnant with Jesus' life, pregnant with the Spirit's power, pregnant with the Father's love through the power of Christ's cross. By learning and living this process, we will then know how to choose God in each situation; we will then find His will.

The following pages give the tools needed for this endeavor. Remember, however, that we must present to God the open-ness of heart and mind that allows these tools to accomplish their purpose.

1

TOOL#1: THE BIBLICAL VIEW

The first tool which must be inspected is an historical one. We need to look at the biblical person's presupposition in relating to God. What was expected? Where was God found? How were God's responses interpreted?

To be concise, we will simply state that biblical men and women (the people of Israel), bound to their God in a covenant experience, held a basic, faith-view of all reality. This stance leads to four assumptions.

ASSUMPTION ONE: God is at work in all believers drawing them to Himself.

The biblical person believed that God was encountered on two levels: in life and in history. She/he was conscious that God spoke to individuals, giving them direction and guidance (cf. Genesis 15:1), and was also attuned to God's voice speaking throughout Israel's history. This latter expectation allowed the believer to hear and see God speaking and revealing Himself in the events of the past.

This insight actually formed the people of

Israel into a unified body. It enabled the individual to be one with all Israel, even when separated by great distances or periods of time. Hearing and responding now became a communal event, as well as an individual event. This insight enabled the biblical person to be there at Mt. Sinai with *all* God's people; to gather for prayer at the temple in Jerusalem with *all* God's people; to bow in worship with *all* God's people — past and present — saying with one voice, "Amen," in answer to the Lord's call.

The realization of this communal and individual relationship with God, opened the biblical person to hear God's Word in every event and situation encountered either as an individual, or as a member of the Israelite community. For example, whether there was defeat or victory in battle, or even a naturally occurring disaster such as famine or drought, it was God speaking.

Such an attitude enabled the biblical person to see God in the existential situation, in the now, as the experience was happening. Whether good or bad, comfortable or uncomfortable, God's Word was being spoken; His word was near, for the listening.

In the process of discernment, the aforementioned assumption should become our own. We need to see God's movement in every situation, bringing all to completion according to His plan. More than simply convincing ourselves that "everything is okay," we must assume that what we experience *now* is God's love for us. St. Paul assures us that everything works for the good (Romans 8:28). For us who acknowledge God's love, this really implies that we are experiencing God's love *now* in the events which surround us.

Such an assumption forces us to discard our own plans. It forces us to give up our hope that in the end God will finally realize our plan was the best. The subtle but misguided self-assurance implicit in this attitude needs to be reshaped within a life of discernment. After all, it is quite easy to accept and believe God's speaking to us and loving us, if we have just received a raise or won the lottery. The loss of a job, the death of a spouse, the pain of an alcoholic child, however, makes it harder to accept the idea that God is somehow loving me and speaking to me in this situation. Yet, for those who believe, the now is God's loving Word for us.

ASSUMPTION TWO: God speaks to us through our intellect (the Old Testament word is, Heart) and affections (emotions).

> For this Law that I enjoin on you today is not beyond your strength or beyond your reach. It is not in heaven, so that you need to wonder, "Who will go up to heaven for us and bring it down to us, so that we may hear it and keep it?" Nor is it beyond the seas, so that you need to wonder, "Who will cross the seas for us and bring it back to us, so that we may

20

hear it and keep it?'' No, the Word is very
near to you, it is in your mouth and in
your heart for your observance.

(Deuteronomy 30:11-14)

This passage points to a basic reality: God's
Word dwells within us ever-present for our
reflection. The Word dwells within each of us —
regardless of our background, our state of life,
our personality. He dwells within to offer
guidance, correction, encouragement, consolation. Using all the events of life, therefore, the
Lord touches our heart and mind. His Word is
constant.

For this reason, we must tune our mind and
heart to God's voice as He speaks within. In
Numbers 11:24-29 we see this directive in opera-
tion. Joshua did not hear God's Word being
spoken because his heart and mind were not
tuned into listening to someone outside his
camp. Therefore, God's Word was missed. In
like manner, we often miss God's Word because
we tune out His voice, should it come from an
unexpected source, e.g. TV, non-believers, world
events, etc. In each of these situations, however,
God's Word is saying something to us, yet we
often ignore it because the source seems too
''worldly.''

To discount these ''worldly'' sources is to
eliminate a body of data in which our mind and
heart are submerged. God is not hiding in the
world, or from the world, making it impossible to
hear Him. He has entered the world so that His

voice can be heard.

ASSUMPTION THREE: Evil is a reality that can work in all.

In today's society, the presence of evil has been sensationalized through movies, books, and news reports. We accept the word, "evil," although we mock the reality. Too often, the stereotype image of the devil with horns and tail has made the reality quite unbelievable. Nevertheless, evil does exist.

Such a statement, however, should not lead us to the other extreme. Although evil is a reality, we must not assume that an evil spirit is behind every tree and the cause of every crisis. More often than not, our own sinfulness is the "evil" present, rather than some personalized demon. The following story helps clarify this point.

> Once upon a time, during the era of princes and knights, castles and serfs, there was a weary traveler seeking shelter for the night. Dusk was approaching and he was rushing to a nearby town before night ended his journey. He did not really want to stay in that town since it had a terrible reputation, but he knew that he needed some type of shelter from the wild animals that prowled the area at night. As night finally came, the traveler reached the gates. Sitting outside, however, was the devil. He knew it was the devil because he had horns and a tail.

Filled with curiosity he asked the devil, "Sir, why are you sitting here, outside the walls. This town has the reputation of being possessed by you. It is known for its evil and violent ways, and you sit here. Why are you not inside the town stirring up the evil for which you are blamed?" Twitching his tail, the devil looked at the traveler, and gave a big yawn. Garbled within the yawn was his answer to the traveler: "They don't need me in there. They're doing very well by themselves!"

By taking to heart these first assumptions, the practical application of discernment will be easier for us. The process itself allows us to be conscious of God's Holy Spirit bearing witness within us through our mind and heart; it helps us to recognize God's Word spoken here and now in the events of here and now; it teaches us how to sense the Lord's presence by recognizing the confirming spirits of peace and joy as each existential event touches us. In short, the biblical person reminds us that the Master's voice can be recognized.

ASSUMPTION FOUR: Discernment is communal.

The biblical person was aware that the entire community was needed to hear the infinitely rich word of God. This community included those past and those present. Perhaps "tradition" best summarizes the biblical attitude.

The Word of God past (tradition) is meant to confirm the Word of God present (the existential event). This takes place because God's word within life and history has been speaking the same message throughout time; that Word dwelling within the community has been saying, "You are Mine, You are loved, You are forgiven!"

For the biblical person and for us, community has an essential place because it reminds us of the basic Word spoken. This is why sharing our heart and mind is important. In doing so, we look to see whether the Word spoken within us is the same as the Word spoken within the entire community throughout all time.

The sharing of which I speak is not the "witnessing" or "major-truth," group dynamic sharing which is often a personal catharsis for the one sharing. The proper "sharing" in the discernment process is our reflection (intellect) on the movement of God's Spirit within (affections) and the comparison of that to His movement within the community (tradition) throughout history. This can easily be done by seeking counsel from a wise person who carries within himself/herself the roots and the traditions of the community, or by engaging in the process of discernment within a group setting. This latter technique will be explained in a later chapter.

To live a life of discernment requires effort. It is a labor, a work in which we need to move wholeheartedly. It requires our learning how to hear things differently, how to listen to others because their words are not merely an opinion, but a gift from God to us now. This work always challenges us to shift gears as new insights, new experiences, new chances for conversion enter our mind and heart through the minds and hearts of others.

Finally, the process of discernment requires that we be freed from our own subjectivity. Here we have the hardest work of all: to be disarmed and defenseless in the Spirit's presence.

PRAYER EXERCISE: Discernment Examen.[1]

This is a simple prayer exercise which can teach us the art of "fine-tuning" our hearts and minds to the promptings of the Spirit. It is not an examination of conscience, which usually helps us to see the rightness or wrongness of our actions. Rather, it is a prayerful inspection of the inner movements and promptings (often called spirits by St. Ignatius) which we have felt during the day.

This type of examen, therefore, will help us recognize what was happening "inside" during those times when we put on the mind of Christ; it will help us to recognize Christ in all things by pointing out how our heart "felt" when we chose or did not choose the Lord. The discernment examen should take approximately ten minutes

[1]This section is taken from notes received during a directed retreat. The notes are by Fr. Armand Nigro, S.J.

when used every night.

1. Relax in the presence of God. Use a psalm or a hymn to help you.
2. Thank Him for everything that He has brought into your life since the day before.
3. *Beg* to be given the mind and heart of Jesus, to see reality as Jesus sees it.
4. Reflect prayerfully over your day by checking the "we" (what you and Jesus experienced together) against the "I" (you alone). This is done in order to bring to life St. Paul's insight "I live not myself alone, but Christ lives in me" (Galatians 2:19). This means that in reality our life is a "we" (you and He) not an "I."

   As you reflect over the day, visualize those events about which you can say "we" (even if you were not conscious of His presence at the time). For example, "We ate breakfast, we drove to work, we cleaned the house, we spent time with people, etc."

   Recall, then, those events about which you cannot say "we." For example, "I blew up at the children, I got angry at the slow traffic, I cheated in the store, etc." As you prayerfully review the day's events in this manner, the Spirit will make you aware of the myriad ways in which He was present to you throughout the day. He will enable you to "discern" or distinguish His touch from all the other movements, promptings and urges in your life. This, in turn, will help you to become more aware of His presence in the days ahead. This awareness will evolve into that ideal of working, playing, resting, living in Him that St. Paul describes.

5. Renew, in love, your sorrow for ever having disappointed or offended the Father. Offer a short prayer of repentance and sorrow at this time.

6. Plan a time of prayer for tomorrow. Make it definite in length and place. Also, promise to repair any damage you may have done to others should He give you the opportunity tomorrow.

7. End by praying the Our Father.

A second prayer assignment is to pray over the Old Testament passage from Deuteronomy 30:11-14. Use the following points for meditation:

1. Begin with a spontaneous prayer asking for the Lord's presence.

2. Reflect on how this passage reveals the mystery of God's plan. Think of how His word is given to us through the Old Testament, the New Testament and in Jesus.

3. Pray for the specific grace to accept the Word. Pray that the Word, as it is embodied and enfleshed in Jesus, will spring to life within you.

4. Think of how the Word is near . . . not beyond you . . . not impossible to live. Let silence predominate. Don't worry about distractions; ignore them.

Think of the different ways the Word has been spoken to you; name the people who bore the Word to you. Ask God to bless them.

Think of the Spirit and how He brought the Word to life for you.

5. Pray to Mary. Ask her intercession, that she who brought forth the embodiment of the Word, she who carried within her person the Word Himself, Jesus, will ask her Son to become part of you.

Pray to Jesus, that He will grant you the grace to become for others, a manifestation of the Word.

Pray to the Father, that He will make you bearer, hearer, and responder to the Word.

6. Slowly pray the Our Father.

7. As a final point of meditation, you might want to listen to the song, "You Are Near."[2]

[2]Taken from the album, *Neither Silver Nor Gold,* by the St. Louis Jesuits. Published and Distributed by North American Liturgy Resources, 10802 North 23rd Avenue, Phoenix, Arizona, 85029. Phone: 1-800-528-6043

2

Heavenly Father, we ask for your blessing.
We know that through the power of your
*   Son, Jesus,*
you have placed within our hearts your
*   Word of Love,*
Your presence in our midst.
Help us to hear that Word;
help us to cling to it with every fiber of our
*   being.*
Help us to know that through the Word
You dwell in us, and invite us to dwell in
*   You.*

TOOL #2: AN EXPLICIT ATTITUDE AND ATMOSPHERE OF FAITH

We are meant to touch and be touched by the reality of the living God: the very same man, Jesus, who 2000 years ago took upon Himself our flesh and our sins. He is alive — not a concept or a myth. We are called to experience Him.

In a life of discernment, our experience[1] of

---

[1]NB Your experience is not necessarily the same as mine, although it is the same God we experience. All valid Christian experiences should somehow resound with the experience of the first witnesses, the apostles.

God is a foundation stone. Not to know Him in the depth of our being, not to know His love, not to know with heart-felt conviction that He is alive — here and now — for me and in me, not to know in some "sensible" way this reality is to begin a life of discernment with severe limitations.

This observation is made, lest we be induced to seek someone false, whose existence for us is hearsay; lest we be persuaded to follow someone we do not know and cannot recognize. Experience of the crucified Lord, raised from the dead, is a necessary first step. Though different in its manifestation in each person's life, this experience or *faith conviction* is essential.

Where, you may ask, does one receive such a conviction? The answer is deceptively simple: from Jesus. The free movement of God towards man is definitively begun in Jesus Christ. As St. Augustine says, "God became man so that man could become God." Supported by a community and nourished with the stillness and quiet of prayer, we proceed with conviction to the God Who already is proceeding towards us, in Jesus.

An individual's faith conviction, therefore, goes beyond the spiritual zap of a cursillo, a charismatic prayer meeting or a "born-again" experience. It rests securely in the pulling, tugging and urging of the Father within our hearts. It is a gift, freely given[2], nurtured in prayer; a gift which may come with sudden power, or subtle

[2]cf. John 6:44; Matthew 11:25-30

gentleness. Regardless of the "way of experience," the fact remains: we know that God is there.

Perhaps, as a child you've had such an experience wherein you strongly felt God's presence and His love for you. Most of us have had such experiences, though they may have slipped our memory. For these experiences to be realized as a faith conviction, we need to nurture them with prayer, whether it be vocal, meditative, or a desperate cry for help. I call this latter prayer the Prayer of the Beggar — offered during those times when we are so low, nothing seems real, so desperate, we are forced to acknowledge that without Him we cannot begin to see.[3]

From this faith conviction emerges a *faith knowledge.* We can have many powerful experiences (Baptism of the Holy Spirit, Marriage Encounter, etc.) but until we begin to grasp a knowledge of Jesus in his humanity/divinity, we remain limited to an undisciplined "feeling." To remain on the experience level (affections) without incorporating the reflective level (intellect) is to play charades. Experience without reflection is useless; it will not sustain life, nor lead us to the God we seek.

A danger of remaining at the level of faith conviction is the danger of seeking experiences of God rather than seeking the God who gives those experiences. It would be like collecting love let-

[3]cf *The Autobiography of St. Ignatius Loyola, with Related Documents.* Translated by Joseph F. O'Callaghan. Edited with Introduction and Notes by John C. Olin. New York, 1974. Section 23.

ters without ever wanting to meet the lover who writes them.

Our thrust in discernment, therefore, is to move with faith conviction to faith knowledge; to come to know with our mind, the Lord we experience in our heart.

This faith knowledge is rooted in Jesus, the Revelation of the Father. As it says in Mark's Gospel, "This is My Son, the Beloved. Listen to Him" (Mark 9:7). *Listening* to Jesus, we learn about the Father; listening to Jesus, we learn the meaning of our heart's experience, which is our faith conviction.

A life of discernment, therefore, requires study. We are not meant to operate from a solely inspirational feeling of God's presence, nor are we meant to rely on our own feelings, thoughts, and ideas. If we disregard faith knowledge as we enter the process of discernment, if we cease learning what the Father has revealed to us in Jesus, what He shows us in our heart's experience, we are doomed to fail; we are inviting chaos, confusion and our own notion of revelation to predominate.

Though Jesus is the definitive and complete Revelation of the Father, God also reveals Himself intimately and personally through our affections. Faith knowledge helps us in this area by showing us how to sift through our emotions, and follow those which lead us to the Father. These emotions (affections) vary in kind and intensity: anger, lust, joy, pride, peace, etc. They need to be clarified, separated and integrated in such a way that they reveal to us a leaning or non-leaning toward the Father.

A difficulty of critical importance encountered today is that of attempting to teach faith knowledge without a faith conviction experience. On the other hand, a problem confronting some Pentecostal groups is the tendency to cling to their faith conviction, but to disregard, as superfluous or unimportant, the whole area of faith knowledge. A life of discernment requires both.

As faith conviction and faith knowledge become integrated, a third level surfaces: *self-knowledge*, or self-awareness. We are now able to answer the question, "Who am I?" since our self-identify can be found in God's revelation of His own self to us in Jesus. To know who I am is to know how I am seen by the Father; to know who I am is to know my name — the name by which He speaks to me.[4] This self-knowledge does not rest on our function in society, or our job description. For example, we are not merely priest, or writer, or parent in the eyes of God. That is our function, not our definition. We are who the Father says we are, namely, His child.

Growth in self-knowledge is important, for with it we can uncover what is going on within our being. For example, as we learn about our sinfulness, we will learn that the Lord frees us from sin; as we learn of our shortcomings, we

[4]cf page 30f.

will learn that the Lord fills the gaps; as we learn "where we're at" in a given relationship or situation, we will learn that God wishes to draw us to "where He's at."

St. Paul states it this way:

> Out of his infinite glory, may he give you the power through the Spirit for your hidden self to grow strong, so that Christ may live in your hearts through faith, and then, planted in love and built on love, you will with all the saints have strength to grasp the breadth and length, the height and the depth; until, knowing the love of Christ, which is beyond all knowledge, you are filled with the utter fullness of God.
>
> (Ephesians 3:16-19)

In this passage he seems to imply that our hidden self, our inner being, must emerge (self-knowledge) so that we might know the love of Christ, which is beyond faith knowledge and faith conviction. This is a growth process which reveals Christ in fullness as our faith conviction and faith knowledge allow the self to emerge.

For this reason we should never be afraid of knowing ourselves, or of asking who we are, in the light of our experience and knowledge of the risen Lord. It is for this reason that acts of penance have always been part of the Church's tradition. In the act of penance, we are able to discover the Lord's plan of redemptive love working through our sinfulness. Penance allows the Spirit of God to strip us bare, so the "real self" can emerge.

To confront our inner self without the Lord, without faith-conviction and faith knowledge, would be a frightening experience. We would find little power within ourselves to change. St. Paul realized this frustration in his letter to the Romans:

> I cannot understand my own behaviour. I fail to carry out the things I want to do, and I find myself doing the very things I hate. When I act against my own will, that means I have a self that acknowledges that the Law is good, and so the thing behaving in that way is not my self but sin living in me. The fact is, I know of nothing good living in me — living, that is, in my unspiritual self — for though the will to do what is good is in me, the performance is not, with the result that instead of doing the good things I want to do, I carry out the sinful things I do not want. When I act against my will, then, it is not my true self doing it, but sin which lives in me . . .
> What a wretched man I am! Who will rescue me from this body doomed to death? Thanks be to God through Jesus Christ our Lord!
>
> (Romans 7:14-25)

By growing in self-knowledge we begin to

realize that the process of discernment, the process of seeking God requires our putting aside everything and everyone.

For how long?	A lifetime.
How much effort?	Every effort.
How can we begin since we have so many other things to do?	We do not have anything else to do except to be stripped, be naked, be dis-armed, be vulnerable so the God who loves us can clothe us with His glory.

Two books that might be helpful in expanding upon this idea of self-knowledge are Corrie TenBoom's *The Hiding Place*[5] and Walter Ciszek's *He Leadeth Me*[6]. These books relate the powerful life stories of a man, and a woman, who discovered that a person cannot be clothed with Christ unless he or she is first stripped naked. This stripping, however, cannot take place if we do not grow in self-knowledge.

As we move from (1.) the experience of God (faith conviction) to (2.) a faith knowledge of Jesus, towards (3.) a knowledge of ourselves (self-knowledge) we begin to grow in wisdom. This helps us to integrate, in the practical situation what we have realized in points one to three above. St. James exhorts us to pray specifically

[5]Corrie TenBoom. *The Hiding Place*. Revell, 1974

[6]Walter Ciszek. *He Leadeth Me*. Doubleday Image, 1975.

for that gift[7] which gives us the ability to "put it all together." St. Luke, however, reminds us that the gift, though freely given still exacts a price.[8]

The reason wisdom "costs," is simple. As we enter into the life process of discernment, as we try day by day to recognize God in our midst, as we attempt to seek Him in every situation, we will be called to follow paths that are unexpected and sometimes undesirable. What foolishness to know where God is and not to go! What foolishness to put off until tomorrow that which we discern the Lord wants today!

When the grace of wisdom is given, therefore, we need to accept it. This is why self-knowledge is crucial. To *know* our weaknesses and strengths, the ways the Lord moves within us as compared to the ways our human spirit or an evil spirit moves within, will help us respond to the wisdom given. In the life process of discernment, wisdom points out the direction, but we ourselves must choose to go there; wisdom will lead us towards the Paschal Mystery, but through our self-knowledge we need first to acknowledge what must be purified.

Another image used in Luke is that of a king going off to battle.[9] He must first know his strengths (self-knowledge) before he can execute the plan (wisdom) which will guide him in the

[7]James 1:5-6
[8]Luke 14:25-29
[9]Luke 14:29-31

37

battle. We, too, must pay the price for wisdom — the willingness to sacrifice the illusion of self as we seek our real self in God.

Part of the inner struggle with living the life process of discernment is not our uncertainty regarding a direction, but rather our uncertainty that the direction chosen will really lead us to the God we seek. Hannah Hurnard's classic, *Hind's Feet on High Places*[10] shows, through a simple allegory, what might occur if we are willing to pay the price — despite the doubts and fears which tell us "No," despite the fact that the Lord's "wisdom" does not always seem that wise.

At this point, everything might seem too "theological" or speculative to be practical or real; it might seem beyond our grasp and comprehension. For this reason, we should "practice" with a prayer exercise so that we can begin to "hear" God's voice, begin to know "who we are" before Him, and recognize His calling us by name.

NAME OF GRACE

> But now, thus says Yahweh,
> who created you, Jacob,
> who formed you, Israel.
> Do not be afraid for I have redeemed you;
> I have called you by your name, you are
> mine.

(Isaiah 43:1-2)

[10]Hannah Hurnard. *Hind's Feet on High Places.* Tyndale House Publishers, Inc., 1976.

38

A way that God speaks to us, both individually and as a people, is through the use of our Name of Grace. To live the life process of discernment, therefore, requires that we know our name — our "nickname" through which God gets our attention. We might call this our Name of Grace. To know this "name" is important in discovering who we are in His eyes, not in the eyes of the world. The world already gives us a name: carpenter, activist, sister, mother, lawyer, etc. That is not the name we want to hear; that is not the name which should give us our definition. We need to hear our real name, our true definition according to the plan of God.

This emphasis on name is rooted in scripture and in our own experience. In the Old Testament, for example, the people were not allowed to use Yahweh's name because Yahweh did not receive His definition or meaning from the people. He was simply He Who is beyond control of His creation. In the New Testament, Jesus changes Simon's name to Peter — the Rock upon which Jesus built the Church.

In our own lives we have seen how important a name can be. Perhaps you have noticed children arguing over a certain decision. Suddenly one child tells the other, "Mommy told me I could do it this way." Suddenly, by using a name, the situation changes. The child wielding the name, "Mommy," now has power and control. So it is with us and the Lord. As we come to know God's name for us, we will have power in the situation because we will see how the Lord is calling us in that situation.

When listening for our personal Name of Grace, we should listen with the heart, not with the mind. To clarify this directive, the lyrics to a song which describes one person's Name of Grace have been printed. By reading the lyrics (or hearing the song) we might get a better idea of what our own Name of Grace might be.

FEAR NOT, THOUGH THE DARKNESS WILL COVER THE SUN FROM YOUR EYES. FEAR NOT, I AM WITH YOU. I'LL ALWAYS BE THERE AT YOUR SIDE.

1. *And I'll show you the way: wisdom I'll place in your heart; and I'll follow you with my eyes free you from all of your anguish, so*
2. *Yes, I'll make you my son. You will be child-of-my-heart. I'll protect you from your oppressors, and I'll heal all of your wounds. Little one,*
3. *And I'll listen to your prayer. When you cry, I'll be there. I will clothe you with peace, and your mourning I'll change to joy.*

Copyright 1979, C. Aridas[11]

My personal Name of Grace is "child-of-My-heart." When I pray, that is how the Lord speaks to me. In the most difficult situations, I am

[11]From the album, *Out of the Darkness*, Aslan Records, Inc., c/o Living Flame Press, Locust Valley, New York 11560.

assured of His presence when I "hear" my Name. This may or may not change the situation; that is not important. All that matters is the assurance that He is there.

To discover our Name of Grace requires patience; it does not come quickly, but usually in bits and pieces. A helpful technique is to inspect our life and see how the Lord has already been speaking to us. The following questions may be of some assistance.[12]

1. What are my favorite images of God? (Rock, Father, etc.)

2. What do I look like because of Him?

3. Who is the God to whom I pray most often: Father, Son, Spirit?

4. Which of God's names means most to me?

5. Under which of His attributes does God most clearly reveal Himself to me?

6. Which are my favorite passages from Scripture?

7. Which beatitude attracts me most? Which gift of the Spirit? Which fruit of the Spirit?

8. What is my favorite liturgical feast?

9. Under what aspect has Christ chiefly presented Himself to me for my loving and faithful response?

Suffering Servant of God

The Eldest of many brothers

High Priest and Universal King

Savior and Redeemer

[12]Taken from the Jesuit Center for Spiritual Growth. Wernersville, PA.

The Alpha and Omega
The Way, the Truth, the Life
The Prince of Peace
Loving Bridegroom
The Living Word
The Risen Lord, etc.

PRAYER EXERCISE: Samuel 7:18-19

1. Ask God's blessing in the preparatory prayer.

2. Think of the mystery of God's plan; remember that He incorporates you into it; that He continues to converse with you, as He continues to hold all things in Himself. Let that privilege lift your spirit.

3. Pray specifically that the Lord will give you the grace to hear your Name of Grace. If the questions above are helpful, use them.

4. Reflect upon the following points:

— Remember your nothingness, except that the Lord has spoken you into existence.

— Recall the many promises that the Lord has made and fulfilled for you already. Let Him remind you of the times He was in your life.

— Make a list of the promises yet to be fulfilled. Pray for the patience to wait with hope.

— Make a "time line" to record the different moments in your life when you saw grace develop. In doing this, you should pray with the attitude that you will receive revelation from the Lord which will enable you to sense where and how He has been working.

5. End with prayer

— Ask Mary to intercede that Jesus will speak clearly to you.

— Ask the help of Jesus in hearing the name His Father has given you. Ask also for the grace to be true to that name. (Remember that you are only who God says you are; to be other than this is to live a lie.)

— Thank the Father for His call; thank Him for the name He has given you; thank Him for His love.

3

As they were eating he took some bread,
and when he had said the blessing, he
broke it and gave it to them. "Take it," he
said, "This is my body." Then he took a
cup, and when he had returned thanks,
he gave it to them, and all drank from it,
and he said to them, "This is my blood,
the blood of the covenant, which is to be
poured out for many."

(Mark 14:22-24)

TOOL #3: PERSONAL ANAMNESIS

In Chapter One we tried to establish the basic
assumptions which would be useful in living a
life of discernment. In describing these "tools,"
we saw discernment as a process which goes
beyond our knowing what to do, or what to accomplish in a particular situation. We saw that
discernment was a life in God — not a God
somewhere "out there" — but One present in our
human experience because of Jesus. All this is a
growth process during which we learn to choose,
on the level of faith, those inner affections which
lead us towards the Kingdom — the place of

44

transformation in Christ.

In addition, we learned that God has singled out our uniqueness by endowing each of us with a "Name of Grace," that special nickname by which we recognize His voice. To discover our Name of Grace requires prayer, silence, discipline, and a desire to see and hear the Lord in our human experiences. These are the initial building blocks needed for entering a life of discernment.

At this point we must look at the third tool needed for a life of discernment. The technical term is personal anamnesis. It is an impressive phrase which simply means remembering. In living a life of discernment, in seeking God and His will, we must learn how to return to our first moments of grace. We might say that we have to remember our roots, our story.

The Church returns daily to its first moment of grace through the Eucharist. Is it not true that through the Eucharist we are at the foot of Calvary; we are at the death of Jesus on the cross? In some way we are there — present — just as John, Mary, and the other women were present.

Personal anamnesis, therefore, is our going back in time and reliving that experience of grace, in our own being. Think of a tree: it grows above its roots but never outgrows them. We, too, are called to grow above our past experiences, whether they be Marriage Encounter, a "born-again" experience, Cursillo etc., although we are not going to outgrow them. This "recalling" allows our past experiences to nourish us in the present just as the roots nourish the tree that grows above it.

One living a life of discernment treasures these graces — not for the sake of seeking or clinging to an experience — but rather for the purpose of becoming refreshed and nourished anew. St. Peter says, "Try even harder to make God's call and choice of you a permanent experience."[1] Our ability to remember is personal anamnesis.

In prayerful reflection we drink anew at the springs of past graces. Entering into the quiet and solitude of prayer, we encounter this gift of remembering, this grace, which bears the mark of eternity. Just as our hearts are filled with joy when we recall a treasured memory, so our past graces remembered refresh us again and again. Perhaps the reason is that Jesus, Emmanuel, God-with-us, Gift of the Father endures forever in His Spirit, for God does not give us His gifts in vain. His gifts do not disappear or evaporate like a mist. They are part of God Himself, the giving of Himself, since all graces spring from Him.

The Gift or Grace from God is Jesus in His Holy Spirit — an eternal presence. Personal anamnesis can help us integrate that eternal moment of God's speaking His Word to us, here and now; it can help us realize that every moment with Jesus is a never ending beginning —

[1] 2 Peter 1:10 TEV

new, fresh, vibrant.

Through this process we are refreshed by allowing our latent knowledge and experiences of God to resurface. For example, why do we reread love letters if not to remember the experience of receiving them and savor them once again in the present? Through personal anamnesis we discover that grace endures; it is eternal because Jesus, the source of grace, is eternal. This is why Jesus is called Emmanuel, God-with-us. He, Who is the unique Gift and Grace of the Father, is ever present with us in His Spirit.

Personal anamnesis is clearly illustrated throughout the Old Testament whenever God's people were called to remember what the Lord had done for them, e.g. the Ten Commandments, the Exodus, the Sinai Covenant. This "remembering" was, in fact, a crucial element in the renewal of the Israelite people. Through it, there was a real participation in the past event by "remembering" it in the present. The Passover Ritual is another example of this mind-set in action.

This should not surprise us. The very idea of past, present, and future which we call time, is something humankind has invented. For God, there is no time, there is only present. What seems past to us is ever-present to Him.

As we enter the process of personal anamnesis, we literally shatter time by stepping outside our own concepts and entering into God-time: the eternal now, where past, present, and future

47

are one point in God. Within our own Catholic tradition we experience this reality. In the Eucharist, we celebrate more than a re-enactment of an historic event; we step into eternity by sharing a moment of the past here in the present.

The same is true for Sacraments wherein Jesus is present now, in the way He was present then, because they are one and the same way, and it is one and the same God who is present. This is true for our liturgical experiences as well.

Grace, therefore, is forever. It is a moment in history that becomes history. It is a moment in time that becomes timeless. This is how Jesus is for us. He is the Word made flesh, the Word of Love spoken in time from the Father's heart. By speaking that Word in time, that Word revealed itself as timeless — ever present to us all.

To enter deeply into a life of discernment, we must learn how to enter into the timelessness of Jesus, ever present. We must learn how to enter the timelessness of God's love, forgiveness, grace, power and Spirit. Through this process, true "renewal" takes place because we draw upon the enduring grace of the Father, already given in the Word Incarnate; we draw from the infinite reservoir of God-with-us.

Those times when we pray for "more grace," therefore, are actually contradictions since the Father has already filled us to overflowing. Our prayer, in reality, is a prayer to respond to the grace already present. Through personal anamnesis we are aware of this truth, and so reflect upon the past in order to enter the eternity of the present moment.

PRAYER EXERCISE: To become proficient in using this tool, the following exercise is recommended.

Try to locate, by memory, those deep reservoirs of grace which spring from our souls, one for each of our deepest religious experiences. Locate any one of these experiences and allow it to flow into the present with its entire composite of feelings, moods, thoughts, convictions, commitments and joys. Such an exercise is meant to *refresh* us, not entrap us in the past. Remember, we are going beyond the concept of time into the timelessness of grace.

This exercise is done effectively after receiving Communion. Spend about twenty minutes engaged in this process. Ask for the specific grace of remembering. The following questions are suggestions which may help you make this contact:

1. My first awakening to the realization that God loves me.
2. My deepest experience of God's forgiveness.
3. The day I first heard God's call to "Follow Me."
4. My most cherished experience of God in prayer.

5. My most intimate experience of God in the Eucharist.
6. The day, the hour I discovered God as my personal Savior.
7. My most wonderful finding of God in nature.
8. My most profound discovery of God in another.
9. My most vivid religious dream.
10. Other experiences too personal to categorize.

End by thanking God for the embrace given to you.

4

*Heavenly Father, we come to you asking for
the grace of obedience.
We know that your Son Jesus beckons us
to live in you,
to be one with you,
to abide in you,
so that we might experience
the fullness of life found in your Son.
Help us to hear that call,
and respond to it.
Soften our hearts until we are pliable
in your loving hands.
Open our ears to your voice which says,
"Come, you are mine."
Father, we thank you
for giving us the means to this end
through the loving power of your Son,
present to us in His Spirit.*

TOOL #4: OBEDIENCE

Through a life of discernment we realize our
need for wholeness (or holiness), if we are to find
the God we seek. Wholeness, however, does not
come automatically. There is first the need to

recognize our brokenness. The reason is obvious: if we do not know brokenness, we would think we were whole. If we thought we were already whole, we would not seek wholeness — we would not seek God.

Unfortunately, many people "realize" their brokenness but then, seek God, the problem solver, rather than God, the healer of brokenness. It is unfortunate because God did not come to solve our problems, He came so we could enter His life. Through the Incarnation, He already entered our life; now, we are called to complete the process by entering His.

To live a life of discernment, therefore, is to live our life in Him. He, alone, is the one alive; not you nor I. In fact, we can be considered alive only to the degree that we are alive in Him. This is what discernment shows us: seeking wholeness of life by being alive in Jesus. Perhaps we might look at it this way: in all of creation, there is only one person who is really alive — Jesus the Lord. He, alone, is raised from the dead, living vibrantly and intimately in the Father. Not to be alive in Him, therefore, is to be dead!

This is why St. Paul writes, "You leave behind the old and the new one has come." Who is this new one if it is not Jesus? We are called to put on Christ, to become him, to enter Him.

Discernment, therefore, allows our hearts' need — our need for oneness with Jesus — to be realized through our apprehension by God. We find God, therefore, to the degree that this process takes place. Then, in finding Him, we will know His will.

What is his will? To be His — totally His. He wills that we be completely consumed by the fire of His love. God wants us to return to the natural beauty of his creation.

How? One word sums it up: obedience. We may be frightened by that word, because we misunderstand its meaning. Some people actually avoid using the word when referring to marriage, or authority, or the Gospel's teaching. They think its use implies blindness, foolishness, lack of self-worth on the part of the one obeying.

In fact, however, the word is quite beautiful and meaningful. It tells us "to listen to." The type of listening implied, however, is unlike the listening you expect from a private in the army. It is far more subtle and gentle. In its root, the word means "to give ear to; to strain in hearing what is being whispered on the other side of a wall." Obedience means to give ear to someone's heartbeat; to place our ear on his/her chest and quietly count the heartbeats.

Obedience for us, then, is our listening to the Father's heartbeat; listening to His desire for us; listening in silence with head, heart, and faith mingled together. Through this obedient stance, two levels of communication will emerge: the prophetic word, and the existential word. Together, they can indicate for us the Word of God spoken here and now.

THE PROPHETIC WORD: In the process of discernment, the prophetic word goes beyond the "charismatic gift" often manifested in prayer meetings; it goes beyond a mere foretelling the future, or speaking in the first person.[1] Provided those words are in accord with Church teaching and scripture, they should be pondered with head and heart joined by faith. However, in a life of discernment, the more important prophetic words are "spoken" in the lives of our saints: the Mother Teresa's, the John XXIII's, the Dorothy Day's, etc. Though these "spoken" prophetic words tend to leave us uncomfortable, they are powerful words from God because they strip us of our compromising views of the Gospel and reveal the naked Word of God, in all its power and glory — actually working in their lives.

These prophetic words must be heard and acknowledged if we are to enter the life process of discernment. Though they may make us uncomfortable, though they may seem "beyond us," though we try at times to rationalize their challenge, they need to be heard and obeyed.

THE EXISTENTIAL WORD: This "word" is the one encountered every day: the now word heard on TV, read in the newspapers, etc. In a sense, it is a sign of the times, there for all to see.

As with the prophetic word, we are to sift, separate and differentiate, when the existential

[1]For a detailed explanation of the "charismatic gift" called prophecy, consult *Concerning Spiritual Gifts* by Donald Gee. Gospel Publishing House, 1972

word is heard. It is not an absolute truth — just as the prophetic word is not an absolute truth. By looking at how this "now" word harmonizes with Scripture and teaching of the Church, then by joining it to the prophetic word spoken in the lives of the saints among us, we will have a good idea of what God is saying to us now.

The following example shows this process in action. Newspapers, government agencies, people all around us, sense that things are getting worse in our economy: prices are skyrocketing, goods are becoming scarce, money is getting harder to save. This is the existential word. On the other hand, we hear the prophetic word: people striving to live in small Christian communities, people, like Dorothy Day, living a life of radical poverty and working for the poor. Put these two words together and we "hear" God saying that believers will have to learn how to live with less and share more.

There are three areas where we might hear the prophetic and existential word.

Prayer: This refers to the contemplative type of listening, the pondering, wherein the Word can be heard. Mary, who pondered the message of the angel, is an example of this prayer. Helpful in this area is the daily discernment examen, which was explained in a previous chapter. The proper, inner attitude, therefore, goes beyond "praying." It is an attitude of the heart.

Spiritual direction is also helpful in realizing

this prayer: the guidance of a wise person who can say to us, "It's good, but not God," someone who can help us understand what we are hearing.

In this prayer context, four things should happen: we should become *aware* of what is going on within our spirits; we should learn how to *articulate* what is going on (faith sharing); we should be able to *accept* it as part of a process working within; and, we should choose to *act* one way or another, according to our inner movements.

Hearing the prophetic and existential word, therefore, will bear fruit as we ponder and integrate these four a's into our lives. Mother Teresa remains our example. She first had to be *aware* of what was happening within her spirit — the promptings of the Spirit which led her to her vocation. In addition, she needed to be aware of the needy people around her — those crying out for Jesus. Her awareness, however, had to be expressed, it had to be *articulated* so others could also sense what was occurring. Having realized it was from the Lord, she had to *accept* the process taking place within. Once this acceptance occurred, *action* followed — she chose to work for the poor of India.

Talents/needs: God's grace is specifically tailored for each person. From the universal gift of Jesus and the Spirit comes the unique, specialized grace offered to each individual. It is quite true that grace builds on nature, which is why God's grace is so perfectly suited for each of us. God has placed within our nature various talents and needs which, when touched by grace, will fulfill us and lead us to Him.

For example, we may become aware of certain needs we have, such as the need to be in a Christian community. When we accept this need as coming from God (i.e. it is not an evil desire, or one that would lead us from the Lord), the Lord, Who placed it there, will use it to bring about His plan for us and others. St. Ignatius "needed" to live in unity with his brothers, hence the formation of the Society of Jesus. Charles de Foucauld "needed" to live in poverty, hence the start of the Little Brothers of Jesus.

Perhaps a widow or widower realizes she/he "needs" companionship. Nothing is wrong with this need; it does not imply a weakness or a deficiency. With faith in God, that person might look and see how this need could be used by God — perhaps through the formation of a St. Monica's Club. Although we may not think we have the ability, our "need" may reveal our ability.

Environment: The life of discernment will bear fruit only as we look at our surroundings: the people, things, cultures in which we are situated. If, for example, we have a wife and four children, it is unlikely that God's Word to us will be to enter the Trappists. It may seem like an outlandish example, but everyone has experienced those "strong leadings" which challenge us to move in unusual directions. Or, perhaps, we are living in a posh neighborhood. It is unlikely that the Lord would ask us to open a soup kitchen. The environment does not warrant such a response. He may ask us to sell what we have, or to feed the poor, etc., but the environment needs to be considered, when planning any active response to the Lord.

CHRIST CRUCIFIED
IN THE SERVICE OF OTHERS

What is the common denominator or criterion? John 15:12-13: "Love one another as I have loved you. A man can have no greater love than to lay down his life for his friends." Restated, one might say, "Christ crucified in the service of others." The Christ crucified, however, is not the Christ who has already died for us; the Christ crucified is the Christ who dwells within — the Christ *in me,* crucified for the service of others.

We are meant to do as Jesus did. He saved others by his death on the cross. When speaking of God's will, therefore, when speaking of seeking Him alone, this becomes the common denominator: being stripped, so others can be served. Only when this process can take place, should we proceed in a particular direction. When it cannot take place, we should stop, look, and listen again.

HOW DO WE COME TO THIS
KNOWLEDGE?

A basic principle in a life of discernment is to begin with what we know, moving from clarity to clarity. By beginning with obedience, for example, we will then experience "light," clarity. As is said in Isaiah 55:3: "Come to me; listen, and your soul will live." Through obedience, light emerges.

The "light," which we experience, will then lead us to truth. Jesus says it clearly in John 8:12: "I am the light of the world; anyone who follows Me will not be walking in the dark; he will have the light of life." Jesus does not say, "I am *a* light," but "I am *the* light." Anyone, sinner or saint, who follows, will know the light; anyone, who is obedient, will know the truth.

John 8:31-32 points out that this Truth, Who is Jesus, will lead to freedom "If you make my word your home . . . you will learn the truth and the truth will make you free." This freedom is not to be identified with license. It is, rather, the freedom to be His, the freedom to worship Him, the freedom to accept His embrace. It is the freedom to look at the world shrouded in darkness and say, "No," and to look toward Jesus the Light and say, "Yes."

Such freedom comes as we have grasped the Truth and been grasped by the Truth. Such freedom comes when we see the Light and follow. Such freedom comes as we choose to act: "Would you bring in a lamp to put it under a tub or under the bed?" (Mark 4:21). In this, the choosing to act, the response of love towards others, we find God.

Throughout a life of discernment the Holy

Spirit is working. His job? To re-mind us of everything; to take our mind and make it new; to re-shape and re-form us. The old (mind) is gone and the new (Christ's mind) emerges. Of what does He remind us? He reminds us of the Father's love and forgiveness; He reminds us that Jesus dwells within and that we are freed by His blood. He reminds us that we are His and His alone.

Besides moving from clarity to clarity, we come to this knowledge by uncovering God in all creation (Romans 8). In that discovery, we also realize that all which we encounter is not necessarily God's will. This may seem to contradict previous remarks. However, a life of discernment reveals that though our present experience is the best for us and can lead us to the Kingdom, not everything we experience is necessarily sent by God to take us to the Kingdom.

It may seem a subtle distinction, yet it remains important. Some experiences lead us to the Father because of His marvelous ways and His mercy, not because they are "good" experiences as such. We are bombarded by many experiences, some good, some bad. To assume that God forces us to endure some of them, denies our freedom to choose and respond to them. Better for us to say that God uses all experiences to draw us to Himself.

A death in the family. Did God plan it so we would experience tragedy? Our spouse loses a job. Did God arrange it to see how we would act? More than likely, the answer is, "no"; more than likely our training says, "yes." The fact is, however, that God uses these experiences to bring about the best, and because He uses them, they are the best. A contradiction? No. Merely the mystery of God's love in our midst — light and darkness, death and life.

We must realize, then, that He will grace us here and now by giving us the ability to go to Him. We find Him in our response. For example, a person who loses a job can respond with anger and depression, blaming God, or she/he can respond with searching and hope, trusting that the Lord is holding and loving him/her. The first response sees a curse, and does not see God — though verbally God is "accepted"; the second response sees a gift, not yet discovered.

An important distinction, then, is how are we present to God (our response), not how is God present to us. Too often, we simply say, "Praise God," bow our heads in pious submission and deny the reality of our pain and doubt. Such an approach will not help us to find God; such an approach is not discernment. How we respond in the situation is what leads us to God. Denial of the reality merely denies the God within the reality.

God is already present to us. That is the fact. How He is present will be covered in a later chapter. For now, we will focus our attention on our presence to Him, our response to Him in everyday situations. A life of discernment helps us to perceive these ways of responding by entering the lifestyle of Jesus on the level of faith. St. Ignatius is a guide here because his personal experience was one of pondering the different "spirits,"[2] feelings, and ways he felt God was present to him. By responding in the proper direction, he found (or lost) God.

TOOL #5: INTERIOR FREEDOM

In order to answer the question, "How are we present to God?" we must be free. To help in checking our "freedom level," several areas have been listed for reflection. Remember that no one person is free in any or all these areas. Our entire life is the process of continued dying to self so that the freedom we seek may be realized.

1. Given our stronger inclination toward one choice rather than another, are we willing to accept the possibility that even the choice toward

[2] "Spirits"
When using the word "spirits" we are not speaking exclusively of evil spirits, i.e. personal beings which have been traditionally linked with Satan and his band of fallen angels — although the word does not exclude that possibility. In the broader definition, however, we are speaking of internal spirits, i.e. our affections, human feelings, desires, etc. Jealously, for example, would be a type of "spirit" in this context, since it is an inner movement which leads us in a particular direction. Joy, anger, lust, peace, etc., are other examples of "spirits" in the life of discernment.

To know and name these "spirits" is important because they *move* us toward or away from Jesus. For example, once the "spirit" of jealousy is named and acknowledged, we can realize the freedom of choosing our response rather than the frustration of feeling forced to respond. By choosing to reject or accept the direction in which the inner "spirit" is leading, we can grow in strength and holiness and find God.

which we are less inclined might be the Word of God addressed to us here and now? In short, are we willing to admit that what we want may not be what God wants?

2. Have we consciously or unconsciously dismissed any of our possible choices as a means of fulfilling the goals God has set for us? This often crops up when we are being prayed with for the Baptism of the Holy Spirit. Very frequently a person will pray for any gift the Lord wants, except tongues.

3. Do we fully intend to follow God's Word even before it is discovered, or is our decision and enthusiasm suspended until it is known? This is crucial. Too often, we want to see if "God's will" strikes our fancy before we decide to follow it.

4. Do we really believe that God is concerned in the matter to have a Word to speak, or do we think that He is completely indifferent to any alternative that might be chosen? Do we really believe that God cares?

5. Do we distrust our merely human efforts to find our goals and to utilize the means to achieve them? We need to be on our guard, lest we think that God does not use human means to accomplish His end — remember that Jesus is human. He became human so that the goal of the Father might be achieved.

6. Do we believe that others associated with us are truly willing to be led by God and are sincerely trying to be open to His Spirit? Can we

trust?

7. Does our mistrust of God, or others, or even ourselves make us fearful, timid and cautious in the search and choice of alternatives?

8. Can we commit ourselves beforehand to the discerning groups' final choice (unless it is disconfirmed by just authority or by our own experience in carrying it out)?

9. Are we indifferent to *all* except that to which God is calling?

10. Are we ready to counter, by intense prayer, any desire we might hold which could impede or block the Word of God?

11. Can we accept the fact that God might not choose to speak through the most humanly efficient agent or process to make decisions?

12. Are we willing to name, own, and examine our thoughts, emotions and feelings in order to assess the possibility of self-deception in discerning God's Word?

13. Are we aware of past failures, our lack of freedom and our ever present need for conversion and purification?

14. Are we aware of our fears and ready to renounce them?

PRAYER EXERCISE #1: Read Romans 8:28-30.

1. Offer the usual preparatory prayer.

2. Think of the mystery of God's plan for you; that what you experience is the best for you now; that you are held in the arms of a loving Father

Who will never abandon you.

3. Pray for the specific grace to see the best in life, no matter what circumstances may be confronting you. If there is a particular situation on your mind, focus on it.

4. Points for meditation

— Imagine how disoriented and frightening your life would be if the Lord had not called you His own.

— Reflect on the ways you are the image of Jesus — not the ways you are supposed to be an image of Him.

— Thank the Lord for healing you through His Cross and Resurrection. Thank Him for sharing His glory with you, the glory of his death and Resurrection.

5. Final prayer

— Pray to Mary, asking her for the grace you need to accept the Lord in your life, as she accepts the Lord in her life.

— Pray to Jesus, asking Him for the grace to allow you to enter more completely into His life.

— Pray to the Father in heaven for the above graces.

6. End with the Our Father

PRAYER EXERCISE #2: Reflect upon the points regarding Interior Freedom. Pray specifically for the grace needed to gain a particular freedom you find lacking in your life.

5

PREPARATION FOR DECISION-MAKING

A life of discernment is the ongoing process of our life in Jesus. During this process, there will be times when decisions and choices must be made. This action of decision-making is, in fact, no more than an intensified period of prayer within a prayer process already in motion. To think, therefore, that a person suddenly decides to discern is rather misleading, especially if the life process of discernment is not being lived.

Experience has shown that the decision-making aspect of discernment, i.e., the choosing "yes" or "no" in a particular situation, becomes easier as the life of discernment permeates our everyday routine. This is quite reasonable since the actual decision-making time is nothing more than our focusing on those inner movements or forces that are generating and have been generated throughout our life.

The example which comes to mind is that of a magnifying glass. When a person wants to burn a hole in a leaf, she/he focuses the sun through the lens until a flame appears. This technique works when the rays of light are "gathered" on the lens and properly focused on the leaf. If there is no light, or if the focus is incorrect, a flame will not be produced. So it is with decision-making in the life of discernment: our life in Jesus (the shining sun) must be focused (the gathering of rays on the lens) in order to produce a decision (the flame).

Think, also, of a cup of tea. No one prepares a cup of tea by placing the tea bag in cold water. Boiling water is needed. So it is with decision-making in our life of discernment: we must be boiling in our life in Jesus (prayer, discernment examen, interior freedom, etc.), if the tea is to be prepared properly.

Patience and perseverance are important. A person cannot decide that she/he will seek interior freedom or a life of prayer in the morning, so that x, y, and z can be decided in the afternoon. The normal, Christian growth process, i.e., dying to self, cannot be bypassed. In fact, the more remote a person is from this growth process of dying to self, the less she/he should presume that God will be perceived in the situation at hand.

THE GIFT OF DISCERNMENT

At this point it might be helpful to distinguish between discernment as a life process and discernment as a charismatic gift. The latter refers to a special charism which graces the entire Church. This charism, or gift of the Spirit, helps a community differentiate between evil spirits and good spirits. Very often, the gift is manifested by an individual within a community framework so that another individual or group will know whether God is or is not moving in a particular situation.

Unfortunately, some perceive the gift of discernment to be a magic formula or pipeline to God. Such people seek out those claiming the gift, in order to "know what God wants." This attitude is dangerous because a person or group can be manipulated without being aware that the gift of discernment is not operating. Just because an individual claims the gift, does not mean that she/he has the gift. "But Father," one might say, "I prayed for the gift. I can tell I have it." Such a conviction is based on inexperience and a lack of understanding. It is the Church (i.e., God's people), that has the gift of discernment. Individuals manifest it according to God's plan, to the degree in which they are living a life in Jesus, not by the persistence of inner voices, special signs, or intense feelings.

The signs indicating the validity of such a gift have been stated before: allegiance to Scripture and Church teaching, willingness to die to self in the service of others, and a life-style centered in the Lord.

Properly used, the gift of discernment enables the individual or group to see the Lord's actions in a particular situation, thereby allowing a choice to be made. This gift, however, is not meant to brow-beat or pressure a person into submission; it is not meant to manipulate or force an issue because "God has told me." The gift, properly used, respects the integrity of the other by avoiding debate or clever maneuvering.

In summary, we might say that the gift of discernment is used by an individual for another person or group, while a life of discernment is that growth process through which all believers learn how to choose the Lord in their daily lives. The gift may operate as a unique grace given in a time of need for an individual's or group's growth, while a life of discernment is a process that does not rely on extraordinary moments of illumination.

THREE ASSUMPTIONS
FOR PROPER DISCERNMENT

1. While gathering and inspecting the data needed for the decision-making process, we assume that the entire community is needed to hear the infinitely rich Word of God. This "community" reaches beyond our prayer group, parish council, family, etc. It includes the Christian community through all time.

The Father has spoken one Word to us. That Word, Jesus, is the same yesterday, today, and tomorrow. Throughout all ages this Word existed and then, in time, was made tangible for us in the Incarnation. This is why we need the entire community to hear the Word; this Word of God — Infinity become flesh. We might call this "community hearing," our tradition, i.e., how our community has responded to the Word through time.

69

Thinking that we, individually, can hear that Word in the vacuum of our lives is to deceive ourselves. Only by listening with all God's people — the saints through all time — can we be sure that our hearing is "tuned in." God does not speak in an individualized vacuum; He speaks to a people, calls a people, forms a people. To seek Him, therefore and to know His will is to know how He has spoken to His people, and then to compare our own inner "words" or calls to those already spoken in history.

This does not negate or deny the fact that God "speaks to us" as individuals. It simply places everything within the proper framework: community. For example, in speaking to Moses, God spoke to the Israelite people; in speaking to Mary, God spoke to His bride, the Church; in speaking to the saints, God spoke to peoples everywhere for all time. To remain in our own little corner believing that we have single-handedly "discerned" God's Word is quite foolish and dangerous.

2. Decisions made during a life of discernment should always be consonant with the nature of the group or individual. In other words, we cannot choose to go where we are not allowed. For example, an individual feels the Lord is telling him/her to sell the house in which she/he is living. However, the house is not his/hers; it is rented. In such a case it would be easy to see that the Lord was not telling that person to sell his/her house! On the other hand,

upon further reflection, that individual might realize that the Lord was encouraging him/her to share what she/he does own.

In decision-making, therefore, one must stay within the proper sphere of competency. It is exciting to decide something upon which we cannot act (leaving our family to become a monk in Tibet) while we avoid those very areas in which we should act (reading Scripture one half hour each day).

Implicit in this assumption is that decision-making in a life of discernment is something we do for ourselves — or for the group of which we are a part. We alone must choose the action we will take; others should not decide for us. Lawful authority and tradition are present to confirm the validity of our choice, by keeping us rooted in the community's experience; they are not present to remove decision-making from our lives. The input they offer is meant to clarify the choices possible, not to remove our freedom of choice.

Within the Church, and within its many movements of enthusiasm, e.g., charismatic renewal, marriage encounter, etc., there remains the danger of people's willingness to give up their responsibility to choose for themselves. This is done with all sincerity, believing that others (in authority) are meant to choose and decide for them. This is not meant to be. Tradition and lawful authority are called upon *to help us decide* properly, i.e., choose the Lord and His Kingdom in every situation. No one is meant to force that decision. To do so would be to take away the chance for growth which each choice and decision for the Lord usually brings.

We, as a people, are probably more comfortable when told what to do, rather than when encouraged to enter the life of discernment which prepares us to make decisions in light of the Spirit's movements within. The latter approach is hard work requiring prayer, fasting, etc. The former asks only for blindness which ignores the Light within.

This warning is given because "discernment" can be a weapon used by some to manipulate people. We should not, therefore, believe that a "discerning person" is meant to tell us what to do. She/he may be called to clarify the situation for us so we can choose the Lord with more certainty. We, however, must choose to act for ourselves.

A good rule of thumb in this area is to keep all things in the light. Never follow the directions of those "unnamed" groups (the "we" that nobody identifies), which state, "We've prayed and heard God say. . . ." In a similar vein, do not immediately follow the advice of an individual who manipulates with the words, "The Lord told me to tell you. . . ." Such absolute statements need testing against the criteria mentioned in previous chapters of this book.

3. The final assumption is the constant in the process of decision-making within the life of discernment: the glory of Jesus' cross will be re-

vealed. We must remember, however, that it is Jesus' cross which must be glorified — not our own self-imposed crosses. More often than not, sincere Christians accept "crosses" which are not from the Lord. Many people automatically assume that any tragedy, heartbreak, or crisis that might occur is from God, rather than seeing these experiences as part of our human condition. The Lord can and does use these situations, but they are not necessarily His cross, given so that He might be glorified. In deciding the validity of the "cross" in each situation, use selflessness as a sign. Does it call you to be selfless and is it leading you to that reality with joy?

LEGITIMATE EXPECTATIONS IN THE DECISION-MAKING PROCESS

The Presence of the Risen Lord. The first and most important thing to expect is the Lord's presence. As we focus on those inner feelings or "spirits" which are part of our life in Jesus, we can expect Him to reveal His redeeming power and presence. This reality is of far greater importance than any specific answer we may be seeking. In fact, it is not unusual that the reality of the Lord's presence will be the only answer we "receive" while attempting to reach a decision in a difficult or confusing situation. Although we always hope for a clear choice, it may not be apparent at a given time. The Risen Lord, however, will always be apparent, if we are faithful in our life of discernment.

Healing and Forgiveness. Coupled with the power of the Risen Lord is His healing and His forgiveness. By recalling the chapter on interior freedom, we will remember how in the areas discussed, emphasis was placed, not so much on the importance of setting goals for ourselves, as upon the value of recognizing attitudes that need to be healed or forgiven. In seeking a specific decision therefore, we should expect healing to occur both for ourselves and for others.

Forgiveness will also be present. We may be called to accept the Lord's forgiveness or to be His forgiveness for another. Should we create a barrier in these areas, clarity will not emerge and we will find it difficult to make a proper decision.

Wisdom and Prudence. Definitive answers (those true for all time) are never reached in the decision-making process of a life of discernment. In fact, that which is absolutely best is seldom reached. What usually emerges during this intensified period of prayer and focusing is a "leaning towards" the Lord and His Kingdom. We lean towards the response we are best able to give at this time. Hopefully, tomorrow's "best" response will be better than today's "best" response.

Wisdom and prudence point out that our "leaning towards" the Kingdom might change in time depending on our response-ability and the grace of God. The Lord does not demand of us today what we can only do tomorrow.

Included in this assumption is the fact of our sinfulness: our human limitations which cannot be disregarded. Living the life of discernment does not free us from this fact. Only Jesus frees us. Discernment cannot remove from our lives the reality of our fear, our anger, our lack of freedom. Only Jesus does this. This "freedom" is accomplished over the span of our lifetime, through the process of spiritual growth and development.

CONSOLATION AND DESOLATION[1]

Think for a moment of an occasion when the Lord's presence was felt, when a "moving with Him" was experienced. Now, jot down one-word descriptions of your feelings during this time. Do the same with an instance when the Lord was not sensed. If this simple exercise can be done, we will know the meaning of consolation and desolation.

Consolation comes as we move with God. The words normally associated with this experience are joy, peace, power, gentleness, etc. During a time of consolation there is usually an increase of faith, hope, and love. With desolation, however, words such as anger, fear, unrest, anxiety, turmoil, etc., come to mind. In addition, we are not moved towards faith, hope, and love.

In perceiving the difference between consolation and desolation, we become aware of "God's

[1]*The Spiritual Exercises of St. Ignatius.* Translated by Louis J. Puhl, Chicago, 1951. Sections 322-324.

input" in the decision-making process of discernment; we can sense if this Spirit is there, or if we are being led by a different "spirit." While reviewing the cons and pros of a possible decision, do we feel anxious or peaceful, joyful or fearful, etc.? This is the new data the Lord reveals to us, so that we might choose a response which leads towards Him. A computer can methodically list pros and cons; only a person living a life of discernment, however, can recognize and interpret the consolation and desolation that touches his/her inner being.

As we grow deeper in the spiritual life, we will more easily recognize these inner movements. We will notice, for example, how the promptings of a "good spirit" always bring courage, strength, inspiration, and peace, whereas a "bad spirit" brings anxiety, doubts, sadness, and false obstacles. In addition, a "good spirit" will affirm our name of grace and move us to remain faithful to God's call. A "bad spirit," however, destroys our inner integrity and wholeness and presents us with closed doors, with no escape route.

Part of our task, therefore, in the decision-making process of discernment is to be conscious of these inner movements or feelings. Several questions which might enhance our awareness of them are listed for consideration.

1. How do I *react* when I feel angry (or joyful, etc.)?
2. What situations in my life trigger the above

feeling?

3. What signs, within, attract my attention before I respond to the above feelings?

4. How do I feel after I have acted on this feeling?

Journal keeping, and a daily discernment examen will also be of assistance in learning to recognize these signs of God's Spirit.

THREE EXAMPLES BY ST. IGNATIUS[2]

St. Ignatius provides several graphic images in order to help us anticipate the emergence of a "bad spirit" in our life of discernment.

One way to recognize a "bad spirit" is to imagine an angry woman: frenzied, screaming, resentful, agitated. Such are the signs of a "bad spirit," of desolation, and like an angry woman, they must be confronted with courage, lest they rule us against our will. To ignore the angry woman does not make her go away; to ignore the signs of a "bad spirit" does not make it go away either.

A "bad spirit" is also like a false lover who secretly seduces his friend's daughter. Undoubtedly, the false lover would caution the daughter against sharing these encounters with her father. Secrecy, therefore, is a sign of a "bad spirit." It needs to be combated with openness. A spiritual director can help us to develop this openness by relating to us in love, so that we can keep all things in the light, thereby foiling the Evil One.

[2]Sections 325-327 in the Exercises

A third way to recognize a "bad spirit" is by thinking of an army general. In order to capture a city, he would circle about, looking for a vulnerable area. So with a "bad spirit" which will try to attack our area of vulnerability, whether it be pride, or misguided generosity, or laziness, or fear, etc. This is why self-knowledge is a critical factor in combating desolation. By knowing our strengths and weaknesses, we can be prepared for an attack, and not be caught off guard.

PRAYER EXERCISE: Read Mark 10:23-31.

— Begin with the usual preparatory prayer.

— Listen to the song, "Take, Lord, Receive"[3] which is based on a prayer by St. Ignatius.

— Do "Meditation on the Two Standards"[4] a paraphrase of which appears below:

Imagine the scene . . . a large field between two mountains. On either side of the field is an army, each carrying a banner or standard. In the center of the field stands a single person — you.

Look, now toward one side. You recognize it as Satan's army. What does it look like? Satan, himself, sits enthroned on a seat that is red hot with fire and smoke. Try to imagine the harshness, the violence, the anger that emanates from his person. Then, look towards the other side. This army is different in appearance. They are

[3]Taken from the album, *Earthen Vessels,* by the St. Louis Jesuits, NALR, 10802 N. 23rd Avenue, Phoenix, AR 85029.

[4]A standard is a medieval banner which is designed to represent a particular group, guild, or town, etc. See 136-148 in Exercises.

not dressed for war but wear simple garb — they are defenseless and unarmed. Standing in their midst is their King, Jesus the Lord: gentle, simple, attractive in appearance.

Suddenly, amidst cries of pain and shrieks of terror, Satan's army begins to move towards the center. Listen to the noise: the curses, the swearing, the rumble of angry people shoving and clawing their way forward. From the other side, however, comes a different sound: joy, psalms of praise, and cries of gladness arise as Jesus' army moves forward.

As each army approaches, notice the banners they carry. Can you see the words written on Satan's banner? Riches ... Honor ... Pride. Look now at Jesus' banner: Poverty ... Insult ... Humility. Both groups are moving closer; each army is calling out in full voice: "Come, you are mine. Come, you are mine. Come, you are mine."

Suddenly, you notice that you, too, are carrying a banner. Look at it. What does it say? Do you want to carry it, or are you going to thrust it aside because the words mockingly echo Satan's standards (perhaps your banner has lust, work, and manipulation written on it)? Do not despair, for in Jesus all things can be made new. Look again. The banner is blank; you are free to design your own standard. Choose your motto carefully, for the banner you carry indicates the army you have joined.

— Concluding Prayer

— Ask Mary to obtain for you the grace needed to carry the standard of Jesus, first in the highest spiritual poverty, or actual poverty, if it be His pleasure; second, under the banner of insult and contempt; and, third, under the standard of humility.

— Ask Jesus for the grace to be received under His banner. Ask Him to take your banner and change it to one of His.

— Ask the Father for the above graces.

— Pray the Our Father.

— As a concluding song, listen to "I Lift Up My Soul."[5]

A CONTEMPORARY MEDITATION ON THE TWO STANDARDS[6]

We do not need the Gift of Prophecy to realize that the world is in trouble. All the media keep us informed, with mind-numbing regularity, of each new world disaster. Our everyday conversations reveal the personal disasters we suffer. Crisis situations no longer surprise us. We feel, at times, like stunned observers of a holocaust, helpless and afraid.

We have gone through so many "emergencies": the energy crisis, the financial crisis, the hostage crisis. In addition, these have run parallel to other "disasters": the political crisis, the morality crisis, and the nuclear crisis. Problems seem to confront us at every turn. No

[5]Taken from the album, *A Dwelling Place*, by the St. Louis Jesuits, NALR, 10802 N. 23rd Avenue, Phoenix, AR 85029.

[6]This "meditation" is offered as a further point of reflection.

wonder people think that the end is near; it could not possibly get worse! Or could it?

Our governments breed corruption, our cities breed pollution, while family after family succumbs to the social diseases of anxiety and depression. The poor in our midst remain poor; the elderly grow, not only in age but in fear. We who are called to be stewards of God's creation, exploit and rape what He has created.

Nothing seems to work. We have gone through the New Deal, the Fair Deal, the New Society, and the Great Society. Yet, such programs have done nothing more than reveal the depth of poverty and decay that is present. We have gone through wars which were to end all war and built bombs which would halt further bombings, when, in reality we have caused the death of millions because money was spent on arms rather than on people.

Within our very soul we sense this decay. Sexual values and norms, for example, have reached a nadir as seen so graphically on commercial billboards that line our highways: ads that shout "want" and "more" and "better" — fulfill *me*, now. Self-gratification has replaced love and commitment in the same way that the god of military superiority and consumerism has replaced the God of the peacemaker and the poor.

Even our churches bear the rotten fruit sown throughout the world — despite the pockets of renewal which struggle to survive. Multinational corporations are not the only large enterprises that seek power and control over people's lives. For example, in our own communities we see the clergy, prayer group leaders and many others seeking to control and manipulate through a misuse of authority and a misunderstanding of the Law of Love.

We need not pray for a prophetic vision to "see" these things; they are already obvious. In fact, they are so prevalent, we have grown numb, lest we live on the edge of total despair. We have learned to cope by nodding our agreement, by saying, "Yes, it really is terrible. But what can be done?" We have convinced ourselves we are enlightened when, in reality, we stumble about in the dark.

This, then is the question: "Is this the world which God intended? Is this the same world which is called 'good' in the Book of Genesis?" Is the world about us, with its perversion and poverty, its anger and violence, the same world which Jesus made new by His death on the cross?

No! Jesus did not die on the cross so millions could remain hungry and chained by poverty. Jesus did not die on the cross so that children could live on drugs and women destroy the life within their wombs through abortions. Rather, Jesus died on the cross so that we could experience the real world — the world of His Father, the Kingdom, come in our midst, the world touched by His redeeming blood!

The world we know is not that world created and redeemed by God and called "good" in the Bible. The world we experience now is a make-believe world, created by selfishness and pride — our own little "magic kingdom," without the magic. Today's world claims violence and anger, murder and hate, sloth and greed as its permanent denizens. By cautioning us to be in the world but not of it, John is telling us to live in the real world created and redeemed by Jesus; to reject the make-believe world which we ourselves have created.

In his books, *The Chronicles of Narnia*, the very wise Christian author C.S. Lewis shows us what it means to live in the real world. The heroine, Lucy, learns from her friend, Aslan (a lion, who most believe represents Jesus), that she and her companions have chosen a wrong direction for their journey. Only Lucy sees and hears Aslan at this point in the story. Immediately, she tells her companions. Deciding, however, not to follow her advice, because they did not see Aslan themselves, her fellow travelers continue on their own way, encountering many difficulties and hardships. Eventually, they lose ground in their attempt to advance. Weary and exhausted, Lucy begins to cry. Suddenly, she senses a voice, within, calling, "Lucy, come to me." She hurries into the forest and finds Aslan. Putting her arms around him, she cries, "Aslan, why didn't you make them see? Why didn't you speak to them as you spoke to me?" Aslan ignores her questions

and asks, "Did *you* see me and hear what I said?"
"Oh, yes," Lucy replies, "but they wouldn't
listen. I tried to convince them, but they
wouldn't follow." Aslan simply responds, "Why
didn't you follow without them?"

We are called to live in the world Jesus
created and redeemed. The fact that others do
not choose to follow should not deter us from our
course. We must choose again and again to live
in the real world of the Father's forgiveness and
love, the real world of the Spirit's power and
counsel, the real world of the Lord's Kingdom.
Unfortunately, our society attempts to convince
us that its own artificial world is the best possible
one. This is not to be believed. The world our
society has created is not built on Christ: its foundation is pride, greed and lust. This so-called
world has little to do with the Lord, Whose creation is built on love of neighbor and service to
others.

Jesus died on the cross to reveal the deepest
and most profound truth: His infinite love for us.
Outside of that truth there is nothing; outside of
that reality there exists a self-constructed myth
devoid of life and breath. Outside of that reality
is death.

How can we recognize this truth? In answer-
ing that question we must look to the saints. One
of the most outstanding is St. Francis of Assisi, a
poor man who lived simply, sharing everything
he had. He was a man in touch with his God, a
man who communicated freely with the One

Who created him. In addition, he was a man who, tradition tells us, conversed also with God's creation. He talked to the animals, and called the sun his brother, the moon, his sister. Today, we might look upon this as a story of doubtful authenticity, yet, in Jesus' world, nothing is impossible. Just because we, who do not live in the real world, cannot talk to animals, does not mean that St. Francis (who lived in the real world) did not. In fact, we might even say that when we enter the real world of Jesus as deeply as St. Francis did, we too will indeed talk to the animals!

Ignatius of Loyola is another remarkably inspiring saint. He was a soldier, who gave up everything to become powerless in the presence of God; he was a cripple, who walked with grace through the real world revealed to him in Jesus; he was a proud person, who learned submission and love. He was a saint then, and today, one from whom we might learn the ways of the Kingdom.

Think of Mary: simple, trusting, open. She lived in the real world, the world where the Father spoke to His children, the world where the Lord was vibrantly alive; she lived where the Spirit dwelled. So completely did she try to live in God's creation, that God Himself accepted her womb as His world through the Incarnation.

A saint in our own lifetime, is Mother Teresa of India. She is an elderly woman — vibrant, alive in God, poor and holy — who cares for the sick and dying in the streets of Calcutta. There, amidst the worst slum imaginable, with a stench that would drive us back to our airplanes, there in that filth, Mother Teresa lives in the real world; she lives in Jesus' world. After spending her morning in prayer before the Blessed Sacrament, she goes into the streets and brings the dying back to her home where they may die with dignity and peace. We call it heroic and offer her medals; she calls it normal and offers her life. She is living in the real world.

What about ourselves? How can we take up residence in the real world of Jesus Christ, crucified and raised from the dead? First we must acknowledge the "existence" of two worlds; we must acknowledge that conflict exists within our culture and society is telling us a lie. Should we ignore this situation, we will remain deceived, always believing that glass is diamond, that tin is gold, that scraps are the banquet. Ignoring this reality keeps us prey to the intent of the Evil One, who would deceive us with his lies.

His plan of attack ignores no one. He craves control over all people — rich and poor alike. He begins by convincing us to acquire "riches," by tempting us to accumulate wealth of any type in order to be assured of salvation in a crumbling world. In addition, we are "told" that this accumulation will bring us honor. The honor attained, of course, is empty but it is the honor recognized by the world: a larger car, a better school, a second home, etc. As these so-called "honors" increase, we become bloated with pride, which is the most difficult chain to cast off. In three easy steps — riches, honor, pride — we are then led to every other vice. For example, our pride leads to violence because we must defend our riches; this leads to ruthlessness because we must defend our honor, etc.

The plan of Jesus, however, is radically different. He also overlooks no one and speaks His saving gospel to all. First, however, He invites us to embrace the highest spiritual poverty, and, if we are lucky, He invites us to embrace actual poverty. In accepting His invitation, we do not receive accolades and honor, but scorn and contempt. We are called to wear them joyfully because they lead to humility, and when we are humble the Gospel is fulfilled, "The first will be last and the last will be first."

This may not sound very appealing. In fact, our society has told us that such a plan of action is sheer madness. We must not forget, however, the proof of its validity: the resurrection of Jesus from the dead.

When we celebrate the Sacraments, we are called to touch the real world of Jesus — the world of true reality. This is especially true of the Eucharist, wherein we claim the Body and Blood of the Lord as our true center, wherein we claim with certainty, that Jesus is alive in our midst!

Chesterton says, "It is not that Christianity has been tried and found wanting, it simply has never been tried." St. Thomas More, in speaking to his daughter said, "In the end it is not a matter of reason, it is a matter of love." Living in the real world, therefore, is not a matter of reasonableness according to the mind of the world, it is a matter of love acording to the mind of Jesus.

6

THE PROCESS

1. *Prayer.* The process of decision-making always begins with prayer. St. Ignatius urges us to be specific, begging again and again for light and purification. Although the light may seem blinding at first, although the stripping may seem painful, these two graces are needed, if we are to enter the decision-making process properly.

2. *Formulation of the Proposition.* As we pray for interior freedom, we can begin to formulate our proposition. It should concern an important and real matter which is presently at hand. Speculations and intellectualizations must be avoided. Topics for our proposition can cover any area of our life: Should we change our job? Should we work with the elderly? Should we schedule a "hermit" day every month for prayerful meditation and reflection, etc.?

In forming this proposition, we must make a clear, concise and affirmative statement. Commit that statement to writing. As an example, we will use the following proposition: "I propose to spend one full day every month at the parish retreat house in order to fast and pray." A poorly phrased proposition would lack clarity and probably be stated like this: "I propose to pray and fast more each month." When beginning to write, therefore, we should always ask ourselves the "how to's," such as when, where, how, how long, with whom, why, etc.

3. *Gather the Data.* Once the proposition is formulated, we should gather all the information needed to make a wise and prudent decision. To gather the information for the above proposition, the following questions might be asked: How will we get there? Who will take care of the baby? Will our family approve? Does it cost anything? Can we afford it? Will they accept us without a donation? What will we do with the time? When will we begin? What hours will we be absent from home, etc.?

4. *Cons and Pros.* Once the data is gathered, we should move towards intensified prayer, asking, as always, for the specific graces needed to make a proper decision. Then, looking at the information gathered and the proposition formulated, we should list all the cons, i.e., the reasons why this particular proposition should not be followed. This list should be made while in prayer; we should take as long as we need, using as many prayer periods as we feel are necessary.

As the cons emerge from our inner self, we should write them down. Once this is completed we may do the same for the pros, listing all the reasons for acting upon our proposition. The cons are listed first, in order to be free in letting the pros emerge.

How long should this process take? It depends upon each situation. Expecting God to speak within a certain period of time is presumption; deciding to stop after a certain period of time might be good planning!

5. *Sifting and Condensing.* After the cons and pros are listed, begin to separate them according to their order of importance. Each con should be weighed carefully, realizing that some are more important than others. For example, the fact that we might have to skip bridge in order to have our hermit day is not as important a consideration as having to leave our baby unattended for any period of time.

After sifting the cons, proceed to the pros. Eliminate duplication and condense the lists.

6. *Prayer.* Having come this far, continue to ask God's blessing, praying for light and purification. Persevering in prayer, we now inspect our lists, noting what we *feel* as we reflect on the cons and then the pros. We are looking here for experiences of consolation and/or desolation — those inner movements which indicate the Lord's presence. In noting these inner movements, we will have a better idea of the Lord's presence in the situation being considered.

7. *Decision to Act.* Once that "sense" is acknowledged, we should choose to act, since it is in our response that the Lord is to be found.

Remember that a decision to change our course of action should never be made during the feeling of desolation, since that would indicate that the Lord is not present.

After our choice is made, we must pray with diligence that the Lord will confirm this choice, if it is for His greater service and glory. The making of a decision, however, does not eliminate the need for continued humility, for seeking the graces needed to fulfill the choice.

How will He confirm our choice? Through experiences of peace, and inner joy, but most especially through an increased desire and ability to die to self, as we serve others in love.

DECISION-MAKING IN A COMMUNITY — SOME OBSERVATIONS

The process of communal decision-making remains basically the same. In gathering the data, however, a group of people are called upon to add their input. In doing so, each individual should strive to uncover all the necessary data, the "how to's." All possible evidence should be given and clarified, keeping everything in the light. There will be times, of course, when some data cannot be revealed (e.g., items under the seal of confession), but those times are the exception rather than the norm. Holding back data that should be available detracts from the chances of truly choosing the Lord in the situation at hand.

Additional data is gathered *after* each individual has listed his/her cons and pros.

Remember that this initial listing should be done individually without consultation or discussion with others. After each person has his/her list, that list is shared — beginning with the cons — by stating clearly and simply what each person feels the Lord is telling him/her to do. *Each person,* therefore, is asked to share one con (at his/her turn), then the next person is asked to share one con, until all the cons are shared. Should an individual finish his/her list before the others she/he would simply pass, until all the cons are shared. The same is done for the pros. Please note that each person has the responsibility to speak since *this sharing is the new data* available — data given to each person in prayer, hence, data which may be from the Spirit of God.

In sharing this new data (i.e., the sharing of the cons and pros), debate and argument must be avoided. In proceeding from one person to another, simply state, "I feel the Lord is telling us 'no' for this reason." Then *state* the reason and let the next person share. Do not state all your reasons at once lest a person does not share because one individual has dominated.

Such a process is long. With large groups it becomes especially tedious, although variations of the method have been used.

Once the additional data is given, each individual takes his/her list, eliminates duplication, and continues the process at Step Five, that of sifting and condensing.

When it is time for the group to make a decision, they should gather in prayer and state, one at a time, "I feel the Lord is asking us to follow (or not follow) the proposition." There is no discussion at this time; no reasons are given other than each one's personal sense of where the Lord is leading. Once each person has shared, the group will probably discover that the Lord has peacefully leaned everyone's heart in a similar direction.

THE NEED FOR CONSENSUS

In trying to make decisions with others, we must remember that the fastest runners, we might call them prophets — those who see beyond the mountain — may sometimes need to slow down, so that the rest of the group can build up endurance for the journey. This does not mean that an individual should refrain from speaking the Lord's word within the decision-making process. St. Francis of Assisi is a good example. He needed to grow in patience with his small community, often "compromising" because the group's response-ability was less than his own. Yet, interiorly he took giant steps toward spiritual fulfillment growing in wisdom, prudence, and wholeness. Should an individual in a group find his/her "discernment" overruled, she/he should continue to seek the Lord by dying to self in the present situation so that a new dawn might emerge tomorrow.

This does not mean that any individual within a group is meant to go against conscience, lawful authority, Scripture, church teaching, etc. Those are the very parameters within which the group's decision-making process must remain. It does mean, however, that each person should realize and accept the limitations of others; and, that we should not push others forward, but should love them forward, one step at a time in seeking the Lord.

In the initial stages of St. Ignatius' experience, for example, while he and his disciples were deciding on the structure of their society, they all agreed to a particular plan of action. In subsequent decisions consensus was always reached. The time eventually came, however, when this consensus, this unanimity, was not reached. It was then that they realized that a decision could still be made although consensus had not been present. We must avoid, therefore, unnecessary burdens such as waiting for what is not needed.

Should consensus be reached during the decision-making process, thank the Lord. Should there remain an element of dissent, remember that sometimes, to disagree is to be Catholic! Consensus may be God's gift to a group; it may however, stem from our desire to conform. We might all agree because we lack interior freedom, when in reality God wanted some to disagree in order to keep the door open for further growth.

SIGNS OF A SPIRIT-FILLED DECISION

With both individual decision-making, and communal decision-making, the usual signs should be present: internal joy, interior freedom, peace, etc. Should those feelings be lacking the process should be reexamined.

Even when a community lacks consensus, peace will usually be present if the Spirit of God is being followed. This occurs when we are striving to choose the Lord as sincerely as we are able at the time of choice. In such cases, decisions coming from the Lord usually build community, while decisions arising from our human "spirits" usually destroy community. Lack of consensus, therefore, does not imply lack of God's leading. The dissenting voice may in itself be part of the process and plan of God. Saints Paul, Joan of Arc, Teresa of Avila, et. al., are examples of men and women whose dissenting voices became the call to tomorrow's dawn. This can occur because consensus alone is not the sign of God's leading; it is not what makes a community one. The bond which brings oneness and points to the Lord is charity, which covers a multitude of sins and limitations.

In making a communal choice, therefore, remember that we are called in love to carry each other's burdens, the heaviest being the imperfect judgments and half-hearted responses each of us makes when seeking the Lord.

OBSTACLES TO DISCERNMENT[1]

Throughout the time of decision-making in our life of discernment, obstacles of Untruth and Unfreedom will be encountered.

Untruth (Darkness of Mind). Into this category falls any kind of darkness in our life: our human limitations, lack of knowledge, ignorance of the facts, or our inability to collect all the data needed to make a good decision. Very often we are not responsible for these obstacles, yet they are part of our present reality.

A common example of this "darkness" would be our lack of self-knowledge or our poor self-image. Think of the times when we accepted the false definitions thrust upon us by an unbelieving and unloving world: "God can't love me because I'm so rotten" or "I can't do that, I never do anything right." Such slogans bend us out of shape and keep us locked in "darkness" and untruth. To break free, we must seek the graces of interior freedom mentioned in the previous chapter.

A basic "untruth" which stymies the decision-making process is our assumption that a person's goodwill and sincerity automatically removes all barriers. Unfortunately, this is not so. A sincere person may sound quite impressive, but she/he may be sincerely wrong and may be leading in the wrong direction. Truth is needed in addition to sincerity and honesty. Truth alone prepares the correct path upon

[1]Taken from the Jesuit Center for Spiritual Growth, Wernersville, PA.

which we can walk towards the Lord.

Unfreedoms (Darkness of Will). Fear is, perhaps, the most debilitating "unfreedom" which plagues our life. It paralyzes us, making us immobile, tense, and anxious. We fear making mistakes and displeasing our peers. We fear disappointment, suffering and sometimes even love. We fear God's call and what might be asked of us. We fear the radical call of the Gospel and sometimes, we even fear ourselves.

Mixed with this fear is prejudice — our unwillingness to change and/or be changed. Too often, we limit our use of the word prejudice to racial relationships when more frequently, it can be used to describe our lack of openness to deeper truths. The way to recognize prejudice is to look for the "always/never" statement. For example, "The Mass can't be in English because it has always been in Latin" or "Black people never hold a job for long periods of time." This is prejudice at its core: a failure to touch the deeper truth.

Other obstacles to discernment are our unrealistic expectations and assumptions. For example, we expect the Lord to speak to us, so we pray for a moment and then open the Bible in order to hear his Word. This type of Bible bingo carries with it unrealistic expectations. Or, perhaps, our prayer has been dry over the past few weeks, so we assume that God is leading us away from prayer! An unrealistic assumption to say the least.

A common obstacle, one that stems from our misguided sense of prudence, is indecision. By holding off a decision until we are "absolutely certain," we are really deciding not to decide. To feel reasonably assured and to move in faith is generally all that is necessary if we are going to lean toward the Lord. Remember also, we are not deciding infallibly; discernment does not make that boast.

Finally, under the guise of "openness to the Lord" we often erect the obstacle called passivity. "I'll just pray" sums up this attitude. This is the type of "openness" wherein we refuse to take any initiative, just in case God wants to do something else. On the other side of this coin is the person whose "openness" is really a giving in to inner compulsiveness and desires. This type of "openness" is really a barrier to our hearing, seeing, and listening to the Lord.

We should take some consolation in knowing that such "obstacles" are part of normal, spiritual growth. We should not think that we have been "singled out" for punishment, or for attack by the Evil One. They are merely opportunities for us to encounter, in our response, the converting and transforming power of Christ.

TACTICS TO COMBAT THE OBSTACLES[2]

Prayer. Faithfulness to solitary prayer helps us to stop, look, and listen. Through prayer we are led to see the nothingness and lifelessness that exists without the Lord. All forms of prayer are helpful: the petition for interior freedom, the

[2]*Ibid.*

quiet contemplation of Gospel truths, worship and praise through song and tongues, the stillness of centering on God within, etc.

Asceticism. Acts of asceticism are another weapon in overcoming the obstacles to discernment. Basic, physical acts such as fasting will put us in touch with the deepest reality dwelling within and will keep us ever mindful that Jesus alone is the food that satisfies all hunger. Sleeping on the floor, celibacy, and other purely physical disciplines are part of this ascetical arsenal. We must, however, be careful lest we follow a wrong "spirit." Submission to a spiritual guide rooted in Church tradition is a recommended precaution. We must avoid the pious enthusiasm which can easily creep into our spiritual life patterns.

There are other types of asceticism. Psychological asceticism, for example, will teach us how to recognize our fantasies and perceive the areas of our life which need healing. For example, do we know how to deal with destructive thoughts or accusations? Do we "imagine" a full scenario ending with righteous triumph over a person who has harmed us? How to handle such thoughts is the fruit of psychological asceticism.

Almsgiving, Bible reading, retreats, etc., are types of spiritual asceticism which nourish our inner self, thereby strengthening our ability to overcome the obstacles which surround us. Use all these weapons in the battle for purity of heart as you seek the Lord in the decision-making process.

PRAYER EXERCISE

Choose some matter about which a decision is due and formulate a proposition. Keep the statement simple, clear, and positively expressed. If necessary, divide it into two separate propositions for the sake of clarity. The discernment which follows should provide a "yes" or "no" answer to the proposition.

Meditation Song: "I LIFTED MY EYES"

As an opening prayer, you might find the following helpful.

I lifted my eyes to the mountain up above,
and I saw upon the mountain the Savior,
He is Love.

So I left my things behind for He said to travel light,
and He took me by the hand ever upward through the night.

The climb's been long and hard, yet He's never let me go;
and He tells me everyday all the things
I should know.

The journey still goes on for my trust must still increase
if I ever mean to rest forever
in His peace.

I lifted my eyes to the mountain up above,
and I saw upon the mountain the Savior.
He is Love.

[3]From the album, *Out of the Darkness,* Aslan Records, Inc., c/o Living Flame Press, P.O. Box 74, Locust Valley, NY 11560.

7

Heavenly Father
we ask that you place within our hearts
the grace of perseverance,
the grace of long-suffering and patience,
so that our lives may remain focused
on the saving message of your Son, Jesus.
Help us to look neither to the left nor the
*   right,*
but to Him, our source of life and hope.

CHECKING INNER ATTITUDES

At this point, we need to observe more carefully what is happening inside our hearts. Having formulated a proposition and having gone through the cons and pros, we may be experiencing a "what's next" type of feeling. Perhaps we are having some difficulty in trying to figure out what the Lord wants, even though we've already considered the obstacles presented in the last chapter.

Should this be the case, it is time to reassess our intention, to be sure we are seeking *the proper end* result, i.e. seeking union with God. If we are having difficulty in making a choice, it is quite possible that we have not chosen the proper end. Perhaps we are making a means the end. For example, many choose to serve God through marriage (although the service of God is the end). The proper intention is to serve God and then, choose marriage as a means to that end. Some might choose a school or a job in the same fashion, substituting the means for the end.

This distinction is difficult to make because our entire society urges us to choose school, job, spouse, etc., as ends in themselves, rather than first to choose God and let all other choices support this ultimate good. In choosing, therefore, we must make sure that our intention is correct: are we seeking God through a particular choice?

Another reason we may experience difficulty might be that we are not dealing with an important matter or that we are dealing with a subject beyond our competence. The decision-making process will bear fruit only if the subject at hand is good or neutral. For example, we should not "employ" the decision-making process in order to ask the Lord whether an adulterous relationship should be continued. We should not choose to use this method if the proposition is dealing with an unchangeable situation e.g. a marriage which had been validly contracted with faith and interior freedom.[1]

[1]St. Ignatius points out that some "unchangable" decisions lacked true interior freedom when the choice was made. Such decisions should be re-worked within the decision-making process. A vocation choice, not freely made, is not really a vocation or call from God. A perverse choice is never a divine choice. Cf. section 172 in Exercises.

Perhaps our difficulty in choosing stems from the fact that we have already chosen correctly in this matter, hence our efforts are redundant. Should there be doubt as to the correctness of our choice, then the process can be continued.

Sometimes it happens that a correct choice is made for the wrong reasons. When this is discovered, it is wise to choose again so that our response to God is for the right reasons. For example, in entering the seminary to study for the priesthood, I chose that vocation for the wrong reasons. I was substituting the means (becoming a priest) for the end (serving God). It was only after three years that I realized how my initial choice was based on wrong reasons, therefore, I had to re choose my vocation for the right reasons.

Once a decision has been reached, we must remember that the process merely shows us how to "lean towards" the Kingdom. Because of our sinfulness and our human limitations, there is always some lack of interior freedom present when we choose. Even after choosing, we need to allow ourselves time to discover what further purifications need to be made.

St. Ignatius gives several helpful images which can assist us in the process of choosing:[2]

1. When the time comes for a choice to be made, having looked at the cons and the pros, and having sifted through and articulated the spirits of consolation and

[2]Cf sections 185-187 in Exercises.

desolation, imagine a person you do not know. What choice would you encourage that person to make for the greater glory of God and the perfection of his/her soul? You should do likewise.

2. Imagine you are at the point of death. What course of action would you wish to have followed if you could relive the moment? You, then, should now choose that course.

3. Let us now picture ourselves before the Lord of Judgment. Reflect on what decision you wish you had made regarding the proposition presently at hand. This is the decision you should make now.

THREE TYPES OF HUMILITY:[3]

A crucial interior disposition which should be highlighted in the decision-making process is expressed by the word humility. Regular attention should be given to the type of humility that is growing within us, throughout the decision-making process.

The first type of humility is that which is necessary for salvation. It is the most basic type. The person who is humble in this way is willing to be subject to the law of God, and resolves never to disobey that law even if it means death. For this person, mortal sin would never be chosen even if death is threatened.

[3]Cf Sections 165-167 in Exercises

than the first. The person possessing this humility neither desires nor is inclined to have riches rather than poverty, or to seek honor rather than dishonor, or to desire a long life rather than a short one. In short, such a person is *detached;* she/he is not prone to either alternative except to the degree that it helps her/him serve God and allows a dying to self. In addition to these characteristics, the second type of humility also includes a willingness or a resolve not to commit any type of sin: if there were a choice between losing her/his life or committing a venial sin[4] she/he would forfeit life. For example, one might be given the opportunity to advance in business through dishonest means. Humility of the second type would repudiate such a choice.

The third and most perfect type of humility presupposes the first two and then, whenever the glory and praise of God would be equally served, chooses to imitate Christ the Lord.

Choose poverty with Christ, poor, rather than riches; choose insult with Christ, crucified, rather than honor; choose to be counted worthless and a fool for Christ, rather than to be

---

[4]It is important for us to understand correctly the notion of sin. We must remember that the words, "mortal" and "venial" are simply word-constructs used to describe a degree of movement away from God. Be careful to remember, however, that any movement away from God is not desirable. Too often, we think that "venial" sins are okay, while "mortal" sins must be avoided. Avoid the semantics of saying "I've only committed a venial sin." What this really means is that we have damaged our contract with Life itself. Imagine a scuba diver, whose air hose gets narrower and narrower. Eventually, air will no longer reach the diver and his life will not be supported. Venial sin has a similar effect on our souls.

esteemed wise by this world's standards. This third type of humility hearkens back to the meditation on the two standards.

If we are having difficulty making a choice, we may be lacking the proper degree of humility. Does this mean that the third type of humility is needed to make a perfect choice? Yes, that is exactly what it means. Does this mean we cannot make a choice without that type of humility? No, rather it means that we are to choose in the best way possible at the moment; it means we should present ourselves in the best way possible in the "now." The Lord always accepts this offering. Do not be tricked into thinking that step three must be attained before a choice can be made.

A final difficulty in choosing is often seen in our refusal to use the ordinary, Christian means of detaching ourselves from self, i.e. we avoid the "Christ Crucified for the service of others" criterion, described previously. Experience shows us that decisions are more difficult to make if we are afraid of paying the price. This is evidenced by our hope that God will come into our desire, rather than deciding to give up our desire to come into God.

These interior dispositions are combated by prayer. St. Ignatius urges us to pray specifically for the grace to embrace that direction which repels us. If, therefore, we are uncomfortable with a certain type of humility or poverty, we should pray that our hearts will embrace it; we should pray for the courage and wisdom to accept these graces when they are given to us.

Such an approach is not meant to be a type of Christian Masochism that advocates pain because pain is good. Sentimental piety might hold that notion. On the contrary, we are simply advocating the acceptance of Christ's banner, even when uncomfortable. This is a lifetime process wherein we play for keeps. It is not a mental exercise that may or may not work. It is forever. In the context of eternity then, we must remember that the Love of God is our very life; and His love is forever.

Meditation Song:
"YOUR LOVE'S FOREVER"

> To live with all the sorrows that we bear is
>   not easy.
> 'Cause living in a land that's dry to dreams
>   leaves us empty.
> And we're getting nowhere fast.
> Hindered by our wounded past
> Till we call your name at last.
> Your love's forever.
> Your peace endures.
> If we stay here in Your name
> We'll feel the cure.
> You hear us crying
> Our silent tears.
> So we stay as close as fear
> Will let you near.
> To hear each other's constant cries of pain
>   makes us weary.

And bleeding while we dress another's
wounds, leaves us lonely.
Feeling hollow, feeling used,
We're exhausted, and confused.
Still we reach for what is true.

Copyright 1980, Aslan Records, Inc.
& W. Boecker[5]

---

[5]From the album, *Like the Dawn*, Aslan Records, Inc. c/o Living Flame Press, P.O. Box 74, Locust Valley, N.Y. 11560

8

DAY BY DAY[1]

Let's begin with a story: "While living in the palace, Abba Arsenius prayed to God in these words: 'Lord, lead me in the way to salvation.' And a voice came to him saying, 'Arsenius, flee from the world and you will be saved.' Having sailed secretly from Rome to Alexandria and having withdrawn to the solitary life in the desert, Arsenius prayed again: 'Lord, lead me in the way of salvation,' and again he heard a voice saying, 'Arsenius, flee, be silent, pray always, for these are the source of sinlessness.' "[2]

There are three key words for reflection: flee, be silent, pray always. Through the proper integration of these inner attitudes, we will discover a life in the Spirit, which means we will discover our life of discernment. At first glance,

[1]There are three classical writers to whom I am indebted: St. Ignatius of Loyola, St. John of the Cross, and St. Teresa of Avila. Two contemporary authors, without whom I would not have found this framework, are Thomas Merton and Henri Nouwen. I am particularly indebted to Nouwen's articles in *Sojourners,* Volume 9, Numbers 6, 7, and 8.

[2]*The Sayings of the Desert Fathers,* translated by Benedicta Ward, London and Oxford 1975.

these words might imply an "other worldly" spirituality that can not exist in our modern society. In fact, however, this desert spirituality nurtured by these three words, must become our own spirituality lest modern society squeeze us into non-existence.

Flee

A recurring word in spiritual life and growth is solitude. Despite its importance throughout our Churches' experience, however, we continue to ignore its call. The fact, nonetheless, remains: by passively drifting along, and accepting the busy-ness of our society, we are headed for ruin. Our society is not a community, radiant with Christ's love — we may wish it were, but it is not so. Despite our wishing the contrary, our society is a place of domination and manipulation where believers can easily be strangled and crushed. In response to this, we, the children of light, quickly conspire with the darkness. We join the "children of darkness" on their own turf, playing the game with their rules, when, in reality, we should flee and seek solitude.

This is not meant as a condemnation, but as a simple observation. Let's look at our agendas; look at our plans for tomorrow. Are we planning a time for prayer and praise? Are we questioning our activities as to their worth and priority? Probably not. We seldom ask such questions and seldom do we try to answer them! More than likely, our tomorrow is already planned for us and we simply hope, that with our "extra time," we will be able to do those things we "know" are important. Seldom do we look to see if our activity during the day is food for us. We usually assume that certain things must be done, or ought to be done. This approach is not meant to be.

Such an attitude in our day to day routine gives us the first reason we lack solitude in our life: our mis-taken self-identity. We usually rely on our society to define us, to tell us who we are and what is expected of us. Very likely, we want to measure up to those expectations, lest others speak or think ill of us. Our society does not expect us to seek solitude, hence, our moving in that direction threatens our very self-identity. Yet, as mentioned previously, our real self-identity comes from God, not from society. To ignore the call for solitude is to accept a mis-taken self-identity, a self definition not rooted in the Lord.

A second impediment to our seeking solitude is our fear of what we will find. No one wants to be alone, only to discover the inner "spirits" of anger, lust, pride, and greed moving ferociously within. Better to "keep busy" than to acknowledge the existence of such "spirits"; better to avoid solitude completely by sitting back and doing what we want rather than sitting still and doing what He wants. Such an attitude will not lead us to the place of solitude which we are encouraged to seek.

For the Desert Fathers, and for us, solitude is

a place of transformation and conversion; a place where we are weak, vulnerable, and naked; a place where there are no "supports" giving us a false self-identity. In the beginning, solitude is a place of great discomfort because we are forced to meet and fight the enemies within: anger, lust, greed, pride, etc. We have seen these enemies before — denizens of our society, which has found them acceptable — but within, they become unbearable, forcing us to fight or to be defeated. Such a vital process takes place in solitude.

Solitude is the place where we struggle with our confusions and our fantasies — our self-indulgent dreams of power and wealth. Here, in solitude, we discover the truth of our relationships, the reality of our self-deceptions. This place, called solitude is where battles are fought and bruises won; yet, who wants to do battle and become bruised? And so we flee, we do not seek such a place because of fear.

Experience has shown the Church, however, that this battle must be fought: we must discover the enemy within, and enter into the struggle with him/her (the "him/her," of course, being ourself), bearing at all times the Lord's standard and weapons; fighting with boldness and faith, the false self so that the new self may emerge. This takes place only in solitude.

It is absolutely essential, therefore, that we set time aside each day to be alone with the Lord, in this place of conversion and transformation.

Should we avoid such times, we will become victims of a society which hides our true identity in the lies of its anger and greed. By embracing such times, however, we embrace the very place where the Lord Jesus reminds us that we are loved beyond all imagining. So, like the Desert Fathers, we must flee to our desert place.

Be Silent

What should we look for, once we flee? Silence: the practical way in which solitude becomes a reality. Silence: our portable desert which allows us a place of solitude even amidst others. Silence: the quietness of heart which avoids words so that the Word might emerge. Through the practical discipline of silence, we remain in touch with Jesus' world, His Kingdom, while preserving ourselves from the worries, cares, and anxieties that our society has woven into its very fabric. As is said in Proverbs 10:19, "A flood of words is never without its fault."

The Desert Fathers knew the importance of silence. They realized that useless words and conversations sapped their strength, making them citizens of society rather than citizens of the Kingdom. Think of personal experiences and conversations which were mindless, numbing, discouraging, inane; conversations which said nothing and drained us of joy and peace in the process. Silence protects us from such experiences.

A further reason for silence is to guard the

God within; to guard the life of the Spirit. We should, for example, be careful of automatic and/or non-reflective faith-sharing sessions which may be led by a spirit of compulsiveness, rather than the Spirit of Jesus. Our task is to make sure that we do not allow our inner energy to dissipate unnecessarily. Better to say a little than a lot. Remember that a verbal stream of consciousness is not faith-sharing.

In silence, we learn how to speak, because a word with power is a word nurtured in silence — the divine silence in which love and forgiveness rest secure. Remember also, that silence of the heart is more important than silence of the tongue. We would be foolish to think a lack of spoken words indicated a growth in the Spirit, when our heart remained full of wordless gossip and slander. We are fleeing towards a heart-felt silence which embraces the mystery of God's presence in and among us.

Pray Always

There is little sense fleeing, little sense being silent, if we are not praying. The hermits and monks of our churches do not flee and embrace silence for any reason other than their desire to converse with the Word, Jesus, who emerges in silence. They flee to silence for prayer.

While solitude, for the Desert Fathers was being alone with God, praying was their presence to God. In thinking of the exhortation, "Pray always," think first of its Greek root which means, "Come to rest." Praying is our resting in God in the midst of temptation, struggle and pain. It is a resting in God which should be acquired at all costs — even when the body is restless or the world lures us elsewhere, or our inner "spirits" remain apathetic.

In praying always, we are not called to speak a prayer solely of the mind; it is not simply the activity of speaking with God or thinking pleasant thoughts about Him. Prayer is also a "speaking" that springs from the heart in wordless phrases. For example, there are no words which can fully convey the feelings of love and concern we feel for our family. The same is true with God, which is why a silent, wordless prayer is acceptable.

By entering into such a prayer, we are challenged to surrender ourselves to the Lord; we are challenged to hide nothing from Him. Such a prayer unmasks our illusions and false notions about ourselves, helping us to enter into the proper relationship of child to Father. Such a prayer is the prayer of truth and total rest: "Like a child in its mother's arms, as content as a child that has been weaned" (Psalm 131:2).[3] This is the prayer of the heart to which we flee, in silence.

---

[3]Psalm 131:2: Enough for me to keep my soul tranquil and quiet like a child in its mother's arms, as content as a child that has been weaned.

How

The question remains: How, in a hectic day, with a family and two jobs, does one pray this prayer? Church tradition gives us many avenues, all of which are useful. To zero in on only one way, however, is to leave ourselves open to stagnation during times of dryness and desolation.

In the book, *The Way of a Pilgrim,*[4] a Russian peasant shares one such avenue, the Jesus Prayer. He shares the route he took in discovering the unceasing prayer of the heart. Instructed by a Russian monk, he begins to pray the Jesus Prayer: "Lord Jesus Christ, have mercy on me." He becomes so proficient in it, that he is soon saying that prayer several thousand times a day. One day, however, much to his amazement, he discovers that he no longer is saying the prayer with his lips, but with his heart. It had become a part of his very heartbeat. At that moment, we are told, the Russian peasant *began* to pray unceasingly.

Short prayers, ejaculations and Scripture phrases repeated over and over, give us an avenue for unceasing prayer. Any effort expended to incorporate this prayer into our lives will be worthwhile. Such a technique, however, is not meant to be the only way, but one possible way to reach our goal.

In addition, our efforts to bring every aspect of our day into prayer, our efforts to bear the

[4]*The Way of a Pilgrim.* Translated by R.M. French, Seabury Press, New York, 1970.

yoke of Jesus (i.e. the suffering of others), and our efforts to praise Him with words and gestures and songs will help our hearts become transformed into the heart of Jesus. Such a journey is not completed in a moment; it must continue through the boredom and routine of every day before results become apparent.

Throughout this endeavor, we must remember that the liturgy, especially the Eucharist and Penance, are critically important. A Catholic who prays in tongues every day, or says the rosary, or joins his/her heart to the Jesus Prayer, but does not seek food and nourishment through the Sacraments, remains only partially fed.

CONCLUSION

Solitude, silence, and unceasing prayer are critical if a life of discernment is to be maintained. Believe it or not, they help us remain sane and keep us rooted in reality in the midst of a society that is going mad and living in illusion. Solitude, silence, and unceasing prayer will keep us from becoming so distracted by the agonies of these last days, that we fall, together with those we are trying to save.

Finally, this desert spirituality re-models and re-minds us so that we can be living witnesses of Jesus. Then, we will be living a life of discernment because we will be living the life of Jesus present in us.

Is it difficult? Yes, but less difficult than not beginning at all. Is it painful? Yes, but being stripped is always painful. Is it worth the effort? Absolutely, for there is no greater pearl, no greater treasure. Not to seek this is to value nothingness; to finally receive it, is to find Life itself.

We end this chapter as we began, with a story: "There were three Desert Fathers. Every year they made a journey to visit Blessed Anthony — a holy and revered monk. During their times together, two of the Desert Fathers spoke with great relish and enthusiasm to Blessed Anthony. They shared insights, prayers, thoughts and dreams with their beloved monk. The third, however, remained silent throughout, never saying a word. After a long time, Blessed Anthony said to the silent monk, 'You come here often to see me, but you never say a word; you never ask me anything.' The monk replied, 'Father Anthony, it is simply enough for me to see you.' "

This is our goal: to let solitude, silence, and unceasing prayer become so much a part of us, that people will not have to ask any questions; it will be enough for them to see us, because in us they will see Him.

THE TURNING ROAD:
Journey of a Soul   1.95

Ralph Kibildis. Bits of wisdom compiled during the life of a man who was drawn close to the Lord.

PRAY WITH THE PSALMIST   1.50

Sr. Evelyn Ann Schumacher O.S.F. In a series of simple but insightful conversations between God and the psalmist, Sister blends her own prayerful experiences with those of the psalmist as together they move through the lights and darknesses common to all those who truly seek God in prayer.

PRAYING WITH MARY   2.50

Msgr. David E. Rosage. This book is one avenue which will help us discover ways and means to satisfy our longing for prayer and a more personal knowledge of God. Prayer was Mary's lifestyle. As we come to know more about her life of prayer we will find ourselves imitating her in our approach to God.

LINGER WITH ME
Moments Aside With Jesus   2.95

Rev. Msgr. David E. Rosage. God is calling us to a listening posture in prayer in the desire to experience him at the very core of our being. Monsignor Rosage helps us to "come by ourselves apart" daily and listen to what Jesus is telling us in Scripture.

Order from your bookstore or
LIVING FLAME PRESS, Locust Valley, N.Y. 11560

PRAYING WITH SCRIPTURE
IN THE HOLY LAND:
Daily Meditations With the Risen Jesus   2.45

Msgr. David E. Rosage. Herein is offered a daily meeting with the Risen Jesus in those Holy Places which He sanctified by His human presence. Three hundred and sixty-five scripture texts are selected and blended with the pilgrimage experiences of the author, a retreat master, and well-known writer on prayer.

DISCOVERING PATHWAYS TO PRAYER   2.25

Msgr. David E. Rosage. Following Jesus was never meant to be dull, or worse, just duty-filled. Those who would aspire to a life of prayer and those who have already begun, will find this book amazingly thorough in its scripture-punctuated approach.

"A simple but profound book which explains the many ways and forms of prayer by which the person hungering for closer union with God may find him."

Emmanuel Spillane, O.C.S.O., Abbot, Our Lady of the Holy Trinity Abbey, Huntsville, Utah.

THE JUDAS WITHIN
An Interpretation of the Character of Judas and the Judas Within Each of Us.   1.95

Rev. Kenneth J. Zanca. The key message of the book is: Accept the Judas within. In so doing, we confront the incredible mystery of God's love, a love so great that it can embrace the darkness in Judas and in ourselves.

THE BORN-AGAIN CATHOLIC   3.50

Albert H. Boudreau. This book presents an authoritative imprimatur treatment of today's most interesting religious issue. The author, a Catholic layman, looks at Church tradition past and present and shows that the born-again experience is not only valid, but actually is Catholic Christianity at its best. The exciting experience is not only investigated, but the reader is guided into revitalizing his or her own Christian experience. The informal style, colorful personal experiences, and helpful diagrams make this book enjoyable and profitable reading.

MOURNING: THE HEALING JOURNEY   1.75

Rev. Kenneth J. Zanca. Comfort for those who have lost a loved one. Out of the grief suffered in the loss of both parents within two months, this young priest has written a sensitive, sympathetic yet humanly constructive book to help others who have lost loved ones. This is a book that might be given to the newly bereaved.

REASONS FOR REJOICING
Experiences in Christian Hope   1.75

Rev. Kenneth J. Zanca. The author asks: "Do we really or rarely have a sense of excitement, mystery, and wonder In the presence of God?" His book offers a path to rejuvenation in Christian faith, hope, and love. It deals with prayer, forgiveness, worship and other religious experiences in a learned and penetrating, yet simple, non-technical manner. **Religion Teachers' Journal.**

THE PRAYER OF LOVE . . .
The Art of Aspiration   1.95

Venard Polusney, O. Carm. "It is the best book I have read which evokes the simple and loving response to remain in love with the Lover. To read it meditatively, to imbibe its message of love, is to have it touch your life and become part of what you are."
Mother Dorothy Guilbuilt, O. Carm., Superior General, Lacombe, La.

POOR IN SPIRIT:
Awaiting All From God   1.75

Cardinal Garrone. Not a biography of the Mother Teresa of her age, this spiritual account of Jeanne Jugan's complete and joyful abandonment to God leads us to a vibrant understanding of spiritual and material poverty.

DESERT SILENCE:
A Way of Prayer for an Unquiet Age   1.75

Rev. Alan J. Placa. The pioneering efforts of the men and women of the early church who went out into the desert to find union with the Lord has relevance for those of us today who are seeking the pure uncluttered desert place within to have it filled with the loving silence of God's presence.

TO LIVE AS JESUS DID   2.50

Bernard Hayes, C.R. Jesus lived all human experience except sin. This book deals with how He lived out various life situations, using that as a model for all who would be His true followers, and seeks to help the reader to live basic life-events in a Christian way. In simple, everyday language, the author spells out what it means to be a Christian in today's world.

JONAH:
Spirituality of a Runaway Prophet $1.75

Roman Ginn, o.c.s.o. While acquiring a new appreciation for this very human prophet, we come to see that his story is really our own. It reveals a God whose love is unwavering yet demanding, for if we are to experience the freedom of mature Christians, we must enter the darkness of the tomb with Christ, as Jonah did, in order to rise to new life.

ATTAINING SPIRITUAL MATURITY FOR CONTEMPLATION (According to St. John of the Cross)   1.00

Venard Polusney, O. Carm. "I heartily recommend this work with great joy that at last the sublime teachings of St. John of the Cross have been brought down to the understanding of the ordinary Christian without at the same time watering them down. For all (particularly for charismatic Christians) hungry for greater contemplation."
Rev. George A. Maloney, S.J. Editor of Diakonia, Professor of Patristics and Spirituality Fordham University.

WISDOM INSTRUCTS HER CHILDREN: The Power of the Spirit and the Word   2.95

John Randall, S.D.T. The author believes that now is God's time for "Wisdom." Through the Holy Spirit, "power" has become much more accessible in the Church. Wisdom, however, lags behind and the result is imbalance and disarray. The Spirit is now seeking to pour forth a wisdom we never dreamed possible. This outpouring could lead us into a new age of Jesus Christ! This is a badly needed, most important book, not only for the Charismatic Renewal, but for the whole Church.

. . . AND I WILL FILL THIS HOUSE WITH GLORY: Renewal Within a Suburban Parish 1.50

Rev. James A. Brassil. This book helps answer the questions: What is the Charismatic Renewal doing for the Church as a whole? and What is the prayer group doing for the parish? With a vibrant prayer life and a profound devotion to the Eucharist, this Long Island prayer group has successfully endured the growing pains inherent to the spiritual life, the fruit of which is offered to the reader.

GRAINS OF WHEAT 1.95

Kelly B. Kelly. This little book of words received in prayer is filled with simple yet often profound leadings, exhortations and encouragement for daily living.

DISCERNMENT
Seeking God in Every Situation 2.95

Rev. Chris Aridas. Using the wisdom of the Church's tradition, Father Aridas shows how Discernment is within our grasp — indeed is meant to enrich our way of life.

COVENANT LOVE 2.50

Sister Evelyn Ann Schumacher O.S.F. In dialog form, Sister traces the tradition of God's covenant love with man beginning with Abraham and leading to the present day New Covenant, the Eucharist.

LIVING FLAME PRESS
BOX 74, LOCUST VALLEY, N.Y. 11560

Quantity

_____	**The Turning Road — 1.95**
_____	**Pray With the Psalmist — 1.50**
_____	**Praying With Mary — 2.50**
_____	**Linger With Me — 2.95**
_____	**Praying With Scripture in the Holy Land — 2.45**
_____	**Discovering Pathways to Prayer — 2.25**
_____	**The Judas Within — 1.95**
_____	**The Born-Again Catholic — 3.50**
_____	**Mourning: The Healing Journey — 1.75**
_____	**Reasons for Rejoicing — 1.75**
_____	**The Prayer of Love — 1.95**
_____	**Poor in Spirit — 1.75**
_____	**Desert Silence — 1.75**
_____	**To Live As Jesus Did — 2.50**
_____	**Jonah — 1.75**
_____	**Attaining Spiritual Maturity for Contemplation — 1.00**
_____	**Wisdom Instructs Her Children — 2.95**
_____	**. . . And I Will Fill This House With Glory — 1.50**
_____	**Grains of Wheat — 1.95**
_____	**Discernment — 2.95**
_____	**Covenant Love — 2.50**

NAME _____

ADDRESS _____

CITY_____ STATE_____ ZIP _____

☐ Payment enclosed. Kindly include $.60 postage and handling on order up to $6.00. Above that, include 10% of total up to $20. Then 7% of total. Thank you.